High Hats and Harps

LLANOVER: THE SEAT OF THE RIGHT HON. LADY LLANOVER.

Annals and Antiquities of the County and County Families of Wales

High Hats and Harps

The Life and Times of Lord and Lady Llanover

BY HELEN FORDER

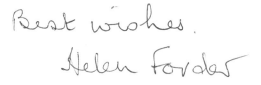

Best wishes.
Helen Forder

TallyBerry PUBLISHING

FIRST PUBLISHED 2012

ISBN 978-0-9570278-3-1

PUBLISHED BY
TallyBerry
United Kingdom

DESIGNED & PRODUCED BY
GLENSIDE PRINTING
WATTSTOWN, PORTH, RHONDDA

Dedication

To Mum for keeping alive the story of
Nanny's high hat and harp.

Acknowledgements

I must first acknowledge the depth of research into the Llanover family by the late Maxwell Fraser. Her articles in the National Library of Wales Journals, and other publications, have been of enormous interest, spurring me on to further research.

My thanks to the many people who have helped, encouraged and supported me during my research, writing and publishing, and my apologies to anyone I have omitted from this list.

Abergavenny Museum, in particular Rachael Rogers and Sally Davis

Brecknock Museum and Art Gallery

Cambridge Harp Association

Falcondale Hotel, in particular Chris and Lisa

Glenside Printing, in particular Kirsty for her brilliant design

Gwent Archives, in particular Tony Hopkins and Frances Younson

Newport Reference Library

Pontypridd Library

Rhes Ganol

S4C

Tinopolis

Llandovery College

Tenby Museum, in particular Kevin Thomas

Mrs Ann Hall, Mrs Sue Hardie, Sanda Lipton, Dr Luned Davies, Catrin Edwards, Mrs June Over, Mrs Olwen Jones, Ms Delyth Clark, Michele Sudar, Moira Harry, Catrin Junyent, Ros Jeffries, John Weedy, Chris Barlow, Keith Floyd, Iain MacFarlaine, Steven John, Terry Evans, Col Rollo Clifford, John Norris, Neil B. Taylor, Michael Freeman, and Mr T. F. James and the family of the late Mrs Gower-Rees. But most of all my gratitude and love to my husband Brian for putting up with my insecurities and my brother Glyn for having faith in me.

Foreword

It is a pleasure to write the foreword to *High Hats and Harps.* My aquaintance with the author arose out of her numerous visits to the search room of Gwent Record Office where I worked as an archivist. Like many of our researchers, Helen's interest was her family's history and while many genealogists are skilled and determined it was clear early on that she was more diligent than most. She soon published an accomplished article in *Gwent Local History* based on her family's connections with the Llanover estate which employed some of her forebears. Her interests widened and if ever an example were needed of how family history can grow into something much larger, this volume is it.

That said, family history is still, in a sense, central to the author's interests in this book. The families in question are those of the Waddingtons and the Halls and the story told revolves around the growth of Llys Llanofer and all it came to represent. Six chapters take the reader on a fascinating social and cultural journey beginning with the arrival of the Waddingtons in Gwent in the late eighteenth century and closing with the death of Lady Llanover in 1896. The marriage of Benjamin Hall and Augusta Waddington in 1823 is the pivotal event in the book for their life together – devoted as they were to one another - provides much of the story's substance. The couple's status rose in 1838 with the baronetcy conferred upon Benjamin, and ascended even further in 1859 when he was elevated to the peerage. Benjamin's death in 1867 ended one of the most fascinating and fruitful marriages in Welsh history. Both partners were formidable and highly energetic. If it is Augusta, *Gwenynen Gwent*, whose contribution is most lauded, the book amply shows that both the Halls championed Welsh culture to the utmost. Benjamin's political career also looms large in the book, and included is a detailed account of the making of the clock-bell Big Ben, which was named after him, in 1856.

The author has made use of a wide range of sources in her book and managed them with skill. It is, indeed, an engaging narrative that gains much of its impact from the fact that its principal subjects are such attractive characters; its success springs equally from the enthusiasm and perceptiveness of its author.

TONY HOPKINS

Let other maids their heads enfold
In tresses dark or coils of gold:
Fair Cambrian maids, believe me that
Your crowning beauty is your hat.

Y CYMMRODOR

Pedr James accompanied by Mrs Gruffydd Richards

Photograph reproduced by kind permission of Monmouthshire County Council, Abergavenny Museum

Had it not been for the patriotic efforts of Lady Llanover, it is probable that
"the distinctive instrument of an old and haughty nation, proud in arms",
would long since have disappeared.

HENRY BRINLEY RICHARDS

Contents

Chapter 1
The Waddingtons of Llanover

Llanover is a parish, in the same division and hundred as Llanellen, about three miles S. by E. from Abergavenny. A railway passes in the vicinity; and in the parish are iron works.[1]

The parish is bounded on the north-east by the river Usk, and the Brecon and Monmouthshire canal runs through it from south to north.[2]

In 1792 Benjamin Waddington[3] 'more from weariness of the long search after a dwelling, than from any temptation offered by Llanover', bought an 'ill-built, incomplete and inelegant dwelling house …'[4] This house was *Tŷ Uchaf* and it was he who styled the elegant house and formed the basis of the lovely parkland to be seen today.

Benjamin and his brother William[5] had established a business in London in 1776 as American merchants, in partnership with Mr Evelyn Pierrepoint. Benjamin went to New York and lived there for several years, as did Mr Pierrepoint, while William looked after the London side of the business. Their business was very successful and in 1784 Mr Pierrepoint retired, followed in 1786 by Benjamin and William who 'resigned their whole business flourishing as it was without any consideration to their brothers Joshua, Samuel Ferrand, and Henry.'[6] Soon afterwards Benjamin retired to the country while William remained in London. Benjamin Waddington, a wealthy, kindly man, married Georgina Mary Anne Port[7] in 1789; she was eighteen years old, and he was forty. At the age of seven this pretty little girl had been taken under the wing of her mother's aunt, Mary Delany,[8] due to her father's financial difficulties.[9]

---

1 Pigot & Co.'s *Directory for Monmouthshire* 1835
2 Kelly's *Directory of Monmouthshire* 1901
3 Benjamin Waddington (1749–1828), third son of the Rev. Joshua Waddington (1711–1780) and his wife Ann Ferrand; born in Walkeringham, Notts. in 1749 and died in Abercarn in 1828
4 *[N]ational [L]ibrary of [W]ales [J]ournal Vol. XI No. 4 Winter 1960* 'The Waddingtons of Llanover', Maxwell Fraser
5 William Waddington (1751–1818), fourth son of Rev. Joshua Waddington and Ann Ferrand
6 Joshua 6th son, Samuel Ferrand 7th son and Henry 8th son of the Rev. Joshua Waddington and Anne Ferrand
7 Georgina Mary Anne Port, daughter of John Port (formerly Sparrow), ?–1807, and Mary D'Ewes; born in Ilam Staffordshire in 1771 and died in Llanover in 1850
8 Mary Granville (1700–1788). Married i) Alexander Pendarves of Roscrow, Cornwall; ii) Patrick Delany, Dean of Down
9 *Mrs. Delany*, Simon Dewes

Georgina's mother[10] was worried about her husband's affairs, which were not in good order, and in 1778 she went to London to visit her aunt, Mrs Delany, taking her eldest daughter, Georgina, with her. She told Mrs Delany of her husband's troubles and it was agreed that Georgina should stay with the elderly lady for a while. From then on Georgina spent many months at a time with her great-aunt, and Mrs Delany greatly missed the company of this delightful girl when she returned to Ilam to spend time with her parents.

Mary Delany was cultured and talented and was one of the most attractive women of her time. She was well connected and during

Mary D'Ewes Port by John Opie
Image reproduced by kind permission of Michele Sudar

her long life had met everyone worth knowing in all circles of society including royalty. She was a prolific letter-writer and showed considerable talent as an embroiderer, an artist and a botanist, being perhaps best known for her 'paper mosaicks', an art form that she created when she was in her seventies. These were pictures of flowers created from hundreds of pieces of coloured paper and were much admired by the leading botanists of the day for their accuracy in depicting nature. Other artistic hobbies were creating decorative pieces from shells she had collected, and cutting out figures in black paper, making silhouettes. She admired the music of George Frederic Handel whom she had met as a child. She had been part of Dean Swift's[11] literary circle in

---

10   Mary Port (née D'Ewes) 1746–1814, daughter of John D'Ewes and his wife Ann (née Granville), Mrs Delany's much loved younger sister
11   Dean Jonathan Swift 1667–1745

Ireland, although she neglected him towards the end of his life.[12] She supported John Opie,[13] Fanny Burney[14] and Hannah More,[15] becoming very fond of the two young ladies. Through her friendship with the Duchess of Portland[16] she became a favourite of King George III and Queen Charlotte and so was able to use her influence to secure a position for Fanny at Court. She enjoyed music, dancing, literature and art and her great-niece was gently encouraged to absorb all this culture as she spent the months with her beloved 'A.D.' [Aunt Delany].

As a result of being taken under her great aunt's wing Georgina had a very privileged upbringing, having been trained by Mrs Delany in 'literary, artistic and social refinement'.[17] She was very much loved and cherished by Mrs Delany and as her

Mrs Delany

Image reproduced by kind permission of Newport Library and Information Services

protégée Georgina mixed in royal circles, becoming a playmate of the royal children, and, when older, helping to entertain the King and Queen when they visited her great aunt. Georgina became a beautiful, flirtatious[18] young woman and unfortunately she fell in love with an elderly equerry. He encouraged her, it seems, but had no intention of marrying her. Fanny Burney, gathering material from the world she saw around her, as was her wont, is said to have based some of her novel *Camilla* on the poor girl's experiences.

When Mrs Delany died in 1788, the future of seventeen-year-old Georgina became a problem for her family. For a while she lived with her uncle, Court D'Ewes,[19] but having been accustomed to the love and kindness of her Aunt Delany her uncle's coldness and neglect made her very unhappy. Some

---

12 *Mrs. Delany*, Simon Dewes
13 John Opie 1761–1807, English portrait and historical painter
14 Fanny Burney (Madame D'Arblay), 1752–1840, novelist
15 Hannah More, 1745–1833, playwright and philanthropist
16 Margaret Cavendish Harley, 1715–1785, m. William, 2nd Duke of Portland in 1734
17 *The Llanover Project: The European Dimension*, Geoffrey Powell
18 According to Fanny Burney
19 Court D'Ewes, 1742–1793; brother of Georgina's mother Mary Port (née D'Ewes)

kindly relatives, sympathetic to her plight, took her to Bath where she met Mr Waddington. Struck by her beauty, he fell in love with her and asked for her hand in marriage. Georgina, grateful for the affection he showed towards her and thinking that no one else wanted her, accepted his proposal.

Benjamin and his new wife first lived at Dunston Park, Berkshire, where Harriet[20] was born in January 1790. The baby survived for only five months and was buried in the churchyard at Thatcham, Berkshire. A second daughter, Frances,[21] was born in 1791. Young Mrs Waddington was said to be very sad, missing her aristocratic and royal friends. According to Frances in her *Reminiscences,* neither of her parents liked the place and they moved to Llanover in about 1792. It seems it was necessary for Mrs Waddington to stay for a while at an Abergavenny inn until *Tŷ Uchaf* was ready to be lived in. Looking back, Frances thought that the house 'needed large additions to be built in order to become a possible place of abode'.[22] It was thought in royal circles that Benjamin Waddington had taken his young wife off to Wales and buried her alive[23] but it is more than likely that Mrs Waddington was visited by some of her new neighbours at this time.

Very soon after their arrival in the area, the Waddingtons made the acquaintance of the Greenly family[24] who had a town house in Abergavenny, land at Llantilio Pertholey and an estate in Cwmdu, Breconshire, as well as their seat at Titley Court, Herefordshire. Their daughter Elizabeth [Eliza] was the same age as Georgina and the two became close friends. Eliza was greatly interested in Welsh culture, she spoke Welsh fluently and no doubt she encouraged her newfound friend to involve herself in the literature and culture of the country that was to become her home.

The Waddingtons frequently read Welsh newspapers and periodicals[25] and welcomed well-known people of the day to their home. Archdeacon Coxe[26] was one who visited frequently while collecting material for his book *A Historical Tour through Monmouthshire* and in it he writes:

'Llanover House, the seat of Benjamin Waddington, Esq., is situated to the

---

20 Harriet Waddington, b. 11th Jan 1790. d. 30th May 1790, buried at Thatcham, Berkshire

21 Frances Waddington (later Baroness Bunsen), b. Dunston Park, Berkshire 4th March 1791, d. Carlsruhe, Baden, 23rd April 1876

22 *NLWJ Vol. XI No. 4 Winter 1960* 'The Waddingtons of Llanover', Maxwell Fraser

23 *The Llanover Project: The European Dimension,* Geoffrey Powell

24 William Greenly, ?–1834, his wife Elizabeth (née Brown) and their daughter Elizabeth, 1771–1839

25 *Cymru* 1908, 'Gwenynen Gwent', L.M.Owen

26 Archdeacon Coxe, 1747–1828, English traveller and author, born in London

right of the high road near the midway between Pontypool and Abergavenny. In this delightful spot I constantly experienced a kind and hospitable reception, and passed much of my time during my continuance in Monmouthshire.'

Members of the Waddington's extended family frequently visited and Welsh literary people, poets and musicians all received a warm welcome.

Why would a wealthy man, with business interests in England and America look at a property in a small Monmouthshire village? Benjamin was obviously a successful businessman, and one supposes that he was well aware of the 'canal mania' that gripped the country at the end of the eigtheenth century. In 1793 the boom in canal building reached its peak, with twenty new canals being authorised in that year. One of these was the Brecknock and Abergavenny canal, the beautiful man-made waterway that passes through the Llanover estate on its

Tŷ'r Bad - Mr Waddington's Boat House Brecknock and Abergavenny Canal

way from Brecon to its junction with the Monmouthshire canal at Pontymoile. So was it just coincidence that Benjamin Waddington bought an estate through which it was proposed to dig a canal? Or was it that, with his keen businessman's instincts, he saw an opportunity to increase his wealth and standing? Supporting this idea is the fact that Benjamin's wife, Georgina Mary Anne Port was the daughter of John Port (formerly Sparrow, a family that had interests in the canals of the Midlands and later in the Brecknock and Abergavenny canal).[27]

In April 1792 Georgina had another child, Mary Anne,[28] but eighteen months later the baby died. Georgina was pregnant again and Emelia[29] was born in February 1794. In 1796 the family spent a short time in Bath, where Georgina's sister Louisa[30] was her companion. Aunt Louisa was much liked by young Frances, because she 'shed a great charm' over her early years. In

---

27 My thanks to John Norris for this information
28 Mary Anne Waddington, born Llanover 16th April 1792, d. Llanover 23rd November 1793
29 Emelia Waddington, b. Llanover 3rd February 1794, d. Llanover 12th April 1819
30 Louisa Port, 1778–1817, m. Rev. Brownlow Villiers Layard, 1779–1861

1797 came visits to Grandfather Port[31] in Derby, and various Waddington re-
lations in Tuxford, Nottinghamshire,[32] Gainsborough, Lincolnshire[33] and
Pocklington, Yorkshire.[34] The stress of all the travelling must have taken its
toll on young Mrs Waddington. She was 26 years old and pregnant with her
fifth child,[35] and on September 23rd Matilda[36] was born. She was baptised on
October 5th but died two days later. Mr Waddington is said to have been in
tears at the death of the baby and Frances too was greatly distressed, especially as her little sister Emelia was too young to understand what had happened and share her sadness. Years later Frances wrote:

[Matilda's] death was a terrible new idea, & caused bitter tears ... —& no
where did I meet with a demonstration of sympathy; so I had an early lesson,
oft repeated in my early life, that sorrow must be borne alone.[37]

During a stay in Bath Mrs Waddington had a morning visit from Prince
Ernest (afterwards Duke of Cumberland and later King of Hanover), an acquaintance from her life at Windsor with Mrs Delany.[38] Frances found these
visits interesting as she enjoyed taking walks in the fresh air, visiting ancient
buildings and meeting a variety of people, but:

The year 1799 ... closed in a manner very distasteful to me, in removal very
late in the season, in the gloomiest of weather, to what seemed to me the gloomi-
est of situations, at Clifton near Bristol, to a house in Gloucester Row, then
looking upon the Downs, at that time very bleak.[39]

Maybe the child was affected by the fact that her mother and small sister were
'always ill' while they were there.

Around the end of the eighteenth century the harvest failed. Mr Waddington arranged for his brother Joshua, then living in America, to send casks of
wheat flour to him, which he sold in small quantities to the needy at cost
price. He spoke to each applicant personally and took great care not to sell to
anyone he thought likely to profiteer by selling it on at a higher price. The

31   Mrs Waddington's father, John Port, formerly Sparrow, died 1807
32   Benjamin Waddington's brother, Rev. George Waddington, 1753–1824, m. Ann Dolland daughter of Peter Dolland
     the celebrated optician. *NLWJ Vol. XI No. 4 Winter 1960* 'The Waddingtons of Llanover', Maxwell Fraser
33   Benjamin Waddington's eldest sister Martha, m. Joseph Hunt
34   Benjamin Waddington's youngest sister Anne, 1745–1826, m. Rev. Kingsman Baskett
35   Only Frances and Emelia survived at this time
36   Matilda Waddington, b. Llanover 23rd September 1797, d. Llanover 7th October 1797
37   *NLWJ Vol. XI No. 4 Winter 1960* 'The Waddingtons of Llanover' Maxwell Fraser
38   ibid.
39   ibid.

minister of Hanover Chapel, known and trusted by all, was often there to translate. Other country gentlemen followed suit and soon a 'Corn Committee' was formed.

Owing to the death of a young cousin[40] in 1800 Mrs Waddington needed to hurry to Bath. Because of the urgency they were not able to make the land-journey in their own carriage 'with all the elegance of a man and a maidservant seated on the driving box'. Frances described their means of travel as follows:

The distance to New Passage[41] was 16 good miles, a regular succession of steeps upwards and downwards: then after crossing the wide estuary of the Severn in a boat – (a navigation in which 'ignorance was bliss' in the opinion of experienced seamen) the travellers proceeded by a hack-chaise & pair of posthorses to Bristol, a drive of 20 miles, & then further in similar conveyance 15 miles to Bath.[42]

Uncle and Aunt Granville,[43] the grieving parents, were invited to Llanover, where they were supported and comforted by Georgina. Other family members also visited Llanover — the Granvilles, the Ports and the Dewes, and the Waddingtons made no more journeys that year.

In the same year Mr Waddington was appointed Sheriff for the county of Monmouth and as Sheriff he was required to escort the Judges to Monmouth. He was preceded by the Javelin-men,[44] chosen from neighbours, servants and labourers, who were dressed in his new livery and riding on horseback. It was characteristic of Mr Waddington that the men he had selected were those who would benefit most from the new clothes rather than those whose appearance as a well matched body of men would have reflected greater glory on the Sheriff himself on his first public outing. Frances recalls the hustle and bustle of the preparation for breakfast on that morning, to which many of the farmers' wives and daughters had been invited. After the procession had left they were 'served & attended to' by Mrs Waddington herself.

An assassination attempt on King George III occurred during Mr

---

40 John Granville, 1779–1800, son of Rev. John D'Ewes, 1744–1826, (who assumed the surname and arms of Granville in 1786 after the death of his maternal uncle, Bernard Granville, last of the male line of Granville) and his wife Harriet Joan de la Bere

41 New Passage was a ferry terminal on the Gloucestershire side of the Severn Estuary. It was closed by Oliver Cromwell after Royalist boatmen left some Parliamentary soldiers to drown; it reopened in 1718

42 *NLWJ Vol. XI No. 4 Winter 1960* 'The Waddingtons of Llanover', Maxwell Fraser

43 Rev John D'Ewes. See note 40

44 Javelin-men, members of a sheriff's retinue armed with pikes who escorted judges at assizes

Waddington's time as Sheriff and he was asked to carry a loyal address from the County to the King, congratulating him on his escape. It was unusual for him to be away from home and it was decided that while he was away Mrs Waddington would take the children to visit her father. By this time Mr Port was living in Derby, his financial circumstances having forced him to move from his beautiful home at Ilam, where Georgina and her siblings had been born. Frances recollects that her father was very emotional, even tearful, at parting from his family, and he gave his young wife careful and detailed instruction as to how to proceed on the journey. It seems to have come as something of a surprise to Frances to realise that Mr Waddington was actually very fond of her mother and the children!

The autumn of 1801 was a quiet time for the family. Mrs Waddington was 'too unwell to leave her sofa' and Frances spent her time reading to her mother, writing letters at her dictation and generally helping in any way she could. Eventually she was told the reason for her mother's illness and general low spirits; another baby was expected, news which made Frances very happy. Many years later she wrote:

I cannot express the joy & delight with which I hailed the baby, which seemed to make me amends for the ever-present first sorrow of my life.[45]

The baby was named Augusta. She was born on the 21st March 1802 and baptised at Llanover on 11th April 1802.[46] She was the last of the six daughters born to Benjamin and Georgina Waddington, and Frances, then eleven years old, was thrilled to watch the development of her little sister.

Baby Augusta was vaccinated against smallpox by Dr. Edward Jenner[47] himself, but the family became alarmed when it resulted in an unusual amount of inflammation, which caused much distress. Dr. Jenner said that if the procedure had not been carried out by himself he would have thought that 'spurious material' had been used.

When Augusta was about 4 months old it was decided that Mrs Waddington would benefit from sea air, and a visit to Sidmouth was arranged. They stopped at Clifton for a day's rest and also at Wells where Frances visited the Cathedral. In her opinion it did not compare favourably with York Minster, which she had already seen. What an exhausting journey for Mrs Waddington

---

45 *NLWJ Vol. XI No. 4 Winter 1960* 'The Waddingtons of Llanover', Maxwell Fraser

46 Llanover Baptisms 1795–1812 no. 149

47 Dr. Edward Jenner,1749–1823, discovered in 1796 that inoculation with cowpox gave immunity to smallpox.
    He called it *vaccination* after the Latin name for cowpox, *vaccinia (from L. vacca, a cow)*

and her three daughters – baby Augusta, eight-year-old Emelia and eleven-year-old Frances.

During that summer the health of the 'precious baby, the joy and idol of every member of the family' gave cause for concern. At first she flourished, being fed by her mother who was fortunate 'in being provided with the means of giving nourishment' but Mrs Waddington was weak and listless and suffered from headaches. She decided to wean the three-month-old baby, but none of the food offered agreed with her. According to Frances 'too many days were allowed to elapse before the experiment was tried of a hired nurse, whom, as being new & unknown Augusta was too intelligent to accept.' There followed a worrying period when the 'treasure of the house' was screaming with pain, unable to digest anything given her, and everyone in the house, including the elderly Mr Waddington, was in tears. One can only imagine the parents' anxiety at the possibility of losing yet another precious daughter.

At last the doctor concluded that the food offered was too rich for the baby's digestive system, and suggested that the quality should be lowered until it no longer caused her pain. So an ass and her foal were purchased and Augusta was reared on the ass's milk. It was 'mixed with three parts water, which had stood upon a hard sea-biscuit, or hard, dry, toasted bread.'[48] Gradually the amount of ass's milk was increased and at last the baby thrived, but was given nothing more substantial until she had enough teeth to bite a hard biscuit.

By the time she was three years old Augusta was showing signs of the determination to have her own way for which she was to become renowned. When the family was staying in London she saw a little girl of her own age wearing earrings. 'The vain little puss', said her mother in a letter to Eliza Greenly, 'has ever since desired to have her ears bored'. Knowing it would be a painful experience Georgina explained to the child that if she really wanted this, then even if the first piercing was painful she must continue and have the second ear done. Augusta decided to go ahead. In a letter to Eliza Greenly Mrs Waddington wrote:

> ... *Augusta was placed on a chair & though she changed colour and trembled, she never shed a tear, made a movement or uttered a cry. Tho' her ear being very fat bled much.*

---

48   *NLWJ Vol. XI No. 4 Winter 1960 'The Waddingtons of Llanover', Maxwell Fraser*

After the ring was put in and the ear bathed, Mrs Waddington kissed the child and then it was time for the second piercing!

> … *so strict a sense of the value of a promise had that child of 3 years and 10 months old, that though she looked very sorrowful, she spoke not a word, but sat still as before. I did not even touch her hands. The poor little thing sat squeezing them together lest she should put them to her head.*[49]

Mrs Waddington, an accomplished and talented woman, undertook her daughters' education herself based on what she had experienced when living with Mrs Delany who was nearly 80 years old when Georgina went to live with her. The old lady had given her great-niece the same sort of upbringing that she had received at the beginning of the eighteenth century and Georgina grew into a charming, accomplished young lady with flawless manners and a strong religious conviction.

Georgina read aloud to her daughters, spoke to them of what she had read and repeatedly told them, 'Whatever you do, do it with all your might',[50] perhaps echoing her great-aunt who declared, 'I like, and love, and dislike with all my might'.[51] Both parents insisted upon utter truthfulness at all times. The girls studied Latin, Greek, Spanish and Italian and were taught music, drawing, history and geography but were also encouraged to play

A Bird Back Excursion

Image reproduced by kind permission of
Newport Library and Information Services

and exercise in the fresh air. Emelia never enjoyed the good health of Frances and Augusta, and despite the eleven years' difference in their ages the two became very close, enjoying each other's company in the more strenuous activities that Emelia could not undertake. The girls had dancing lessons and also learned embroidery and household management. They were taught the art of silhouette cutting, just as their mother had been taught by Mrs Delany.

---

49 *NLWJ Vol. XII No. 4 Winter 1962* 'The Girlhood of Augusta Waddington', Maxwell Fraser
50 ibid.
51 *Mrs. Delany's Menus, Medicines and Manners,* Katherine Cahill

When Frances was about thirteen years old and Emelia ten, a piano teacher from Brecon was appointed to teach them. At the time, Frances was delighted, but years later, in her *Reminiscences* she bemoaned the fact that although these lessons gave her a little knowledge of music, for which she was grateful, she was 'beyond the age when strength and flexibility of finger can be ensured.' She blamed her 'short-coming in music' on the 'want of early & systematic instruction'.

She also mentioned 'the evil influence which presided over' her dress, which seems to have made her unable to show 'a cheerful self-possession in meeting the eyes of others.'

> *Not till after I was married, did I attain to the privilege of choosing & ordering my own dress; & I had at that late date to study & learn with much trouble & under difficulties, that of which the intuitive knowledge ought to have grown up with me insensibly.*[52]

Frances described her family as being 'grave and dispirited', and herself as being 'the only piece of health & activity & comparative cheerfulness.' She seems to have felt no close connection to Llanover, although the family moved there when she was only a few months old, and appears to have had no interest in the Welsh language until later in life. Augusta, on the other hand, loved Llanover and was happier there than in any other place. She considered herself a Welshwoman and was proud of her mother's Welsh ancestors, the Sparrows, linked to the Sparrows of Anglesey, many of whom served as High Sheriff for the county.[53] She was said to have had Welsh lessons and to have run in and out of the tenants' cottages chatting with the people working and living on the estate, who were mainly Welsh speaking at that time, and to have learned about Welsh history and literature from a very early age.

So Augusta grew up in a place she loved, surrounded by a family that loved her; her mother, talented and beautiful, her father, wealthy, kind-hearted and contented and her two sisters to whom she was devoted. The family travelled widely in England and Wales, invited family to visit them at Llanover, and welcomed people like Eliza Greenly and her parents, the Joneses of Llanarth and Clytha and, no doubt, the Halls of Abercarn to their home. They spent the Season in London, where there was a whirl of social engagements – balls, masquerades and dinners, and many friends calling on them.

---

52 *NLWJ Vol. XI No. 4 Winter 1960 'The Waddingtons of Llanover', Maxwell Fraser*
53 *A Genealogical and Heraldic Dictionary of the Landed Gentry of Great Britain.* Sir Bernard Burke.

When in London in 1805, Mrs Waddington met by chance some friends from her days with Mrs Delany, who greeted her warmly. This pleased her enormously as on a previous visit she had not presumed on her previous closeness to them.

> ... as the great-niece of Mrs. Delany, [she] had been on the most cordial and informal terms with the Royal family, but she had so little consciousness of her own charm that on her visit to London in 1803 ... she had made no attempt to reestablish contact with her old friends.[54]

Through these friends, three year-old Augusta and her sisters had their first meeting with Royalty. Queen Charlotte, consort of King George III, sent for them and they met the Princesses.[55]

> Princess Elizabeth took a great deal of notice of Augusta (who says that 'the lady in a blue gown and hoop took her to the window and kissed her')

After a similar occasion during the following Season, Princess Augusta, being asked by the King, 'And who is this little thing?' described four-year-old Augusta Waddington as 'a very beautiful little thing!'[56]

At the end of that Season the family travelled to Tenby, a very risky journey as they had to cross flooded rivers.

> Although they waited for the Tâf to subside, they ladled three quarts of water out of the chaise after the crossing![57]

The 1807 and 1808 London Seasons followed much the same pattern, with Georgina and her daughters being welcomed by her aristocratic friends and being received warmly by the Royal Family.

Privileged though they were, the Waddingtons experienced the same ups and downs of life – births, marriages and deaths – as many another family. There was the marriage in 1803 of Georgina's sister Frances[58] to Abel John Ram[59] and the death of her youngest brother Beville Port.[60] How sad Georgina must have been that it had been through her influence with Prince Ernest that Beville had his appointment to a Cornetcy, which took him to India where he died.

---

54   *NLWJ Vol. XII No. 4 Winter 1962* 'The Girlhood of Augusta Waddington', Maxwell Fraser
55   Princesses Augusta, d. 1840; Elizabeth, d. 1840; Sophia, d. 1848; Mary, d. 1857
56   *NLWJ Vol. XII No. 4 Winter 1962* 'The Girlhood of Augusta Waddington', Maxwell Fraser
57   ibid.
58   Frances Port 1783–1869
59   Abel John Ram 1776–1823
60   Beville Port 1780–1803

There were childhood illnesses such as the very bad case of measles[61] suffered by Frances, after which her mother complained that her previously white complexion had become muddy. Some years later Frances was very seriously ill with typhus. The family's relief at her recovery from this dangerous disease must have been immense.

Following her recovery, the Waddingtons went to Edinburgh where Frances, then aged 19, could benefit from studying under masters[62] and the whole family could enjoy the city's renowned intellectual society. Lady Louisa Stuart[63] sent a letter to Sir Walter Scott recommending her good friend Mrs Waddington to him and his wife, following which Georgina and her daughters were welcomed into his circle. They thoroughly enjoyed their stay, being entertained and in their turn entertaining in the house they had taken. Scott thought Georgina the 'Goddess of Tragedy',[64] her beauty and sadness having made a deep impression on him.

The cause of Georgina's sadness has been attributed to her so-called 'banishment' to the country and to her missing her London and Windsor friends. Maybe this young wife and mother, not in the best of health and having lost three of the daughters she had borne, had other reasons to be sad. When the time came to return home Mr Waddington at least was pleased. Always more content in his own home, he 'certainly was tired of [Edinburgh]' according to his wife.[65] Once back home, Frances studied harder than ever and helped with her younger sisters' education.

Eliza Greenly was a frequent and very welcome visitor to Llanover. A fluent Welsh speaker and an ardent supporter of the Welsh causes of the day, she no doubt encouraged young Augusta's interest in all things Welsh. Frances, although a brilliant linguist, showed little interest in the Welsh language at that time. She had been born in England and considered herself English. Eliza, 'a person of so much real merit, & of such superior & general cultivation of mind', had a good singing voice and on her visits to the Waddington family she would entertain them with her singing, usually the old Welsh folk songs of which she was very fond. According to Frances her voice 'was not of superior quality, but her taste was refined, & she had an admirable collection of songs'. Perhaps it was this early introduction to the old

61 *NLWJ Vol. XI No. 4 Winter 1960* 'The Waddingtons of Llanover', Maxwell Fraser
62 *NLWJ Vol. XII No. 4 Winter 1962* 'The Girlhood of Augusta Waddington', Maxwell Fraser
63 Lady Louisa Stuart 1757–1851, youngest daughter of John, 3rd Earl of Bute
64 *The Llanover Project: The European Dimension*, Geoffrey Powell
65 *NLWJ Vol. XII No. 4 Winter 1962* 'The Girlhood of Augusta Waddington', Maxwell Fraser

tunes that made Augusta Waddington so enthusiastic about Welsh music throughout her life.

Eliza was good natured and attractive and had had a number of suitors but, according to Baroness Bunsen, any man who might have been a suitable husband, and acceptable to her, was 'frightened off from prosecution of his suit, by the ever-increasing demands made upon him as conditions of consent to marriage, by the Mother & Grandmother'. The Grandmother, Mary Brown, was head of the family, 'adding whalebone to Mrs. Greenly's buckram, in all family concerns'.[66] The man Eliza eventually married, in 1811, was Admiral Sir Isaac Coffin,[67] an erratic seafarer who suffered from gout and who was more than ten years older than her. He took the name Greenly on marrying Eliza, heiress to a considerable fortune. Eliza was said to have 'some eccentric habits (such as getting up in the middle of the night to write sermons)' and maybe this contributed to his less than satisfactory behaviour towards her following their marriage. Her behaviour appears to have been without fault, but after the first year of marriage he went to visit friends and stayed away for seven years! He rarely communicated with her and on the few occasions he *did* return, it appears that he was very disagreeable. Eliza once wrote, 'One moment he makes me love him, at another his unfeeling letters and actions completely repel me'. Sir Isaac's relatives and friends sympathised with the long-suffering Lady Coffin Greenly. Eventually he dropped the name Greenly, and Lady Greenly stopped using the name Coffin.

Admiral Sir Isaac Coffin

In 1815 came the news of the end of the Napoleonic wars. Travel on the Continent was once more possible and the following winter found the Waddingtons travelling to Italy. They wanted to reach Rome as soon as possible for the sake of the health of Mrs Waddington and Emelia. It was another

---

66 *NLWJ Vol. XI No. 4 Winter 1960* 'The Waddingtons of Llanover', Maxwell Fraser
67 Admiral Sir Isaac Coffin 1759–1839

busy social time for the ladies, but Mr Waddington as usual preferred the company of his books![68] This was a significant visit for the family as it was in Rome that Emelia, her health greatly improved by the mild climate, met and fell in love with George Manley[69] and Frances fell in love with the penniless young student with whom she read German. He was Christian Charles Bunsen,[70] a serious-minded young man with a great intellect. Eventually Mr and Mrs Waddington were convinced of the suitability of the two young men and gave their permission for the marriages. Emelia was married on 29th June 1917 and two days later Frances married Charles Bunsen. George Manley held an appointment from the Pope and needed to live in Rome, and Bunsen's future was in the diplomatic service, so Mr and Mrs Waddington returned to Llanover with just their youngest daughter to console them at parting from Frances and Emelia.

After their return to Llanover, fifteen-year-old Augusta was her mother's constant companion. She settled to her studies and enjoyed walking and riding in the beautiful countryside surrounding Llanover, visiting tenants and looking after their welfare. Once, when riding out with an English servant as her companion, she heard him say, 'Forty years hence the Welsh language will have disappeared from this country.' Augusta replied, 'If I am living forty years hence, the Welsh language will be here too.'[71]

In the autumn of 1818, Mrs Waddington was pleased to have first-hand news of Frances. On a visit to Exmouth in Devon they met Mrs Drewe, a sister of John Allen of Cresselly, Pembrokeshire. She had spent a year in Rome and had visited Frances almost every day. She had been of great help during Frances's first confinement, for which Mrs Waddington was very grateful and pleased that she could thank the lady in person for befriending her beloved eldest daughter. The Allens were well known to the Waddingtons, sometimes breaking the journey between Pembrokeshire and London to stay at Llanover. John Allen confessed to being more than a little in love with Georgina, and he said had it been possible he would have been 'a fool not to have married her'.[72]

Early the following year Emelia came home. She was very much in love with her husband, but had soon come to the conclusion that her marriage

68 *NLWJ Vol. XII No. 4* Winter 1962 'The Girlhood of Augusta Waddington', Maxwell Fraser
69 George Manley, b. Rome c1792 d. c1861, m i) Emelia Waddington, ii) Sarah Emerson
70 Christian Charles Bunsen, b. Corbach, Germany, 1791 d. 1860. Created Baron von Bunsen in 1864
71 *Cymru 1908* 'Gwenynen Gwent' L. M. Owen. . There is another version of this story
72 *NLWJ 1971 Winter vol.XVII/2* ,' A Pembrokeshire Family in the 18th Century' Elisabeth Inglis-Jones

had been a mistake. George Manley was a Roman Catholic, and although he had never tried to influence her to change her faith she was conscious of the fact that her strongly held beliefs were a barrier between them. She tried to hide her emotions and the fact that her health was deteriorating from her devoted husband and came home to Llanover. Mrs Waddington nursed her herself, not allowing Augusta to help. Augusta's way of easing her mother's burden was to undertake most of the household tasks and try to keep in good spirits. Within a short time Emelia's troubles came to an end. She loved her husband and knew that he loved her, but she welcomed her release. She died on the 12th April 1819 and was buried alongside her two baby sisters[73] in the churchyard at Llanover. *The Morning Chronicle* of Apr 17th 1819 reads:

Died. At 3 O'clock in the morning of Monday last, at the house of her father, Emelia, wife of George Manley, Esq. second daughter of Benjamin Waddington, Esq. of Llanover, Near Abergavenny, Monmouthshire.[74]

This sad episode had a lasting effect on Augusta and possibly accounts for some of her actions in later life.

Life eventually settled down for the Waddingtons and Augusta busied herself visiting and ministering to sick tenants and looking after her various pets. She had a family of goats which she loved, and gave them names such as *Pert Pert* [Pretty Pretty], *Neidwr* [Jumper] and *Caswallon*[75] and had even trained one to pull a little cart in which rode a small cousin! Eventually a dog that she named *Ceidwad* [Keeper] was added to her collection of pets.

On a Sunday in November 1821 a stranger was seen in the village. She was a tall, healthy young woman of about twenty years of age and was carrying a baby. She called at two cottages, where she warmed and fed the infant. In the few hours she spent in the area she no doubt heard of the kindness of the Waddingtons, and at about 7 o'clock that night she left her child 'in such a situation at the door of Benj. Waddington, Esq. that it is wonderful it was not trodden upon!'[76] It was thought that the young mother came from Bristol and had walked from Newport that day.

About a month later the abandoned baby was baptised at Llanover, and was named Maria Lanover.[77]

---

73   Mary Anne and Matilda
74   I am grateful to Peter Stimpson for this item
75   *Caswallon*, British Chieftain at the time of Caesar
76   *The Cambrian*
77   *Llanover Baptisms 1813–1900*, where it is noted that she was baptised on a Sunday

While Augusta and her sisters were growing up in the beautiful surroundings of their home, with the Rhyd-y-Meirch stream tumbling past on its way to join the nearby river Usk, Benjamin and Charlotte Hall[78] and their children had come to live at the neighbouring Abercarn estate which they had been given by Charlotte's father, Richard Crawshay, after he had bought it in 1808. This young family had previously lived mainly in London, with visits to family in Merthyr and Llandaff, and holidays in Swansea, at that time a fashionable seaside resort.

The Abercarn estate was also beautiful, set in the thickly wooded Ebbw valley, and the Hall's eldest son, also Benjamin,[79] grew to love the countryside and the country pursuits at which he became very skilful. Young Benjamin had been educated at Westminster School, where he was admitted at the age of eleven following his time at a private preparatory school. He matriculated on 24th May, 1820 and entered Christ Church, Oxford.

He left there in the Michaelmas term 1821, not having taken a degree.[80] It was during this final term that his mother, by now a widow, married Samuel Hawkins.[81] Benjamin's father had died in 1818. It is not known whether Benjamin and his siblings approved of their mother's choice, and Benjamin never criticised his stepfather, but Mr Hawkins never accompanied his wife when she later visited her children.

After leaving Oxford, Benjamin travelled widely in the United Kingdom, touring North and South Wales in 1821.

The following year, accompanied by his cousin, Richard Franklen,[82] he embarked on a three-month tour of England and Scotland. On 22nd April 1822 the two young men crossed the Bristol Channel from Swansea to Ilfracombe, then travelled over Dartmoor to Plymouth where Benjamin found much to interest him in the Dockyard, particularly the fact that the chain cables were made by 'the Patentee[83] who rents my small iron works at Ynys Llanharad [sic][84] in Glamorganshire'.[85] From there their travels took them to Chichester and on to London. Benjamin soon tired of the socialising and 'the smoke of

78   Benjamin Hall II, 1778–1817, and his wife Charlotte (née Crawshay), 1784–1839
79   Benjamin Hall III, later Lord Llanover, 1802–1867
80   *NLWJ vol. XII, no. 3, Summer 1962*, 'Benjamin Hall's Youth', Maxwell Fraser
81   Samuel Hawkins, of Court Herbert, Glamorganshire, m. i) Sarah Calland
82   Richard Franklen, 1801–1877 [?], only s/o Thomas Franklen and his wife Anne, d/o Richard Crawshay
83   Brown Lenox and Co. Ltd., Pontypridd
84   Ynysangharad, Pontypridd
85   *NLWJ vol. XII, no. 3, Summer 1962*, 'Benjamin Hall's Youth', Maxwell Fraser

London' and decided to visit his friends, the Waddingtons, at their home in Llanover. He was delighted to see them and 'the country, which looks more beautiful than ever'.

When he returned to London the cousins resumed their journey and travelled north through Leicester and Sunderland to Scotland. Benjamin made a point of seeing factories, historical buildings, beauty spots and other things that interested him. One of these was the 'Hanging Bridge' which spanned the river Tweed five miles from Berwick. The bridge, finished in 1820, was the first suspension bridge for vehicles in Britain. It had been designed by Captain S. Brown[86] and 'made at my works near Pontypridd in Wales'.

Armed with letters of introduction from the Marquis of Bute and the Waddingtons the young men had a busy and interesting time and were made very welcome by 'the best society'. They visited such places as Holyrood House and Glamis Castle and went to the Hebrides, the Highlands, and Inverness and were well received wherever they went.

Before they left Scotland they went to Robert Owen's settlement at Lanark where Benjamin was impressed by the happiness of the workers. They were sober, hard working and contented. They had a pride in themselves and in their work, and Benjamin, at the age of nineteen, realised that this was due to 'the proprietor's good sense more than anything else'.[87] The 'company shop' treated its customers fairly, giving full measure at a fair price, but unlike the practice common elsewhere at that time, they were not obliged to buy their goods there. The workers at New Lanark were respected and were paid a fair wage regularly, and they responded by not letting Robert Owen down.

Benjamin and Richard began to make their way south via the Lake District and on to Liverpool. It was there that Benjamin received the sad news that his brother Henry Grant Hall[88] had died. Although he had been seriously ill, the last report Benjamin had received was that he was 'so much better as to be out of danger'. The news caused Benjamin to remain 'for a moment stupefied, hardly knowing what to do', but when the first shock began to recede the young men made arrangements to return home immediately. Although genuinely grieving, Benjamin was ever practical, and rather than sit around miserably waiting for the departure of the coach he used those few hours to visit the Docks which he said later he would have been sorry to have missed.

---

86 of Brown Lenox and Co. Ltd.

87 *NLWJ vol. XII, no. 3, Summer 1962, 'Benjamin Hall's Youth', Maxwell Fraser*

88 Henry Grant Hall, 1810–1822

They travelled overnight, reaching Worcester where they had breakfast and changed their clothes, then sped by chaise to Raglan, from where Benjamin continued his journey to Abercarn. Although the hour was late he broke his journey at Llanover where he was disappointed to learn that his brother had been buried that evening and that there was no one at Abercarn. The tour had covered 2,922 miles and he had travelled from Liverpool to Llanover in twenty-seven hours. His account of the tour ends thus:

We were very much favoured by weather during the whole of our Tour, but the sad occurrence that brought me Home will ever damp the thought of it, which would otherwise be most pleasurable. We returned Saturday, July 20th, 1822'.[89]

In the spring of the following year Benjamin stayed with Lady Greenly in order to take a look at Newport House, Almeley. This delightful mansion is quite close to Titley and is situated in a lovely park with a large lake. Having been taken by Mr Greenly to look it over, and finding it just what he required, Benjamin immediately decided to rent it.

Later that year Benjamin began the preparations for his coming of age celebrations. He enlisted the help of his pretty, vivacious neighbour, Augusta, who entered into the spirit of the occasion with her usual enthusiasm and perhaps her influence can be seen in the decorations of the outside of the hall at Abercarn where the celebrations took place.

On November 8th 1823 the Waddingtons were guests at these celebrations and many hundreds came to witness the event. A dinner for the tenants was held in a large, beautifully decorated room over the New Market Place, Abercarn and they were liberally provided with provisions and *cwrw da*.[90] The room was decorated with evergreens and the front of the handsome building was …

covered with a great number of variegated lamps, some of them forming the letters B.H., with a very handsome transparency of the Goat, and the motto of 'Cymru dros byth; [Wales for ever]' above it and underneath an illuminated Welsh Harp.[91]

There were bonfires and fireworks in the evening, and dancing with Benjamin and his guests joining in 'most heartily'. 'We understand,' said the

---

89 *NLWJ vol. XII, no. 3, Summer 1962,* 'Benjamin Hall's Youth', Maxwell Fraser
90 Literally *good beer*
91 *The Cambrian*

writer, 'that this amiable young gentleman bears a strong resemblance to his late father,[92] not only in his person, but in mind and manners.' The irrepressible Augusta, entering into the spirit of the occasion with her usual zest and sense of fun, composed some verses supposedly written by one of the Abercarn tenants. These were written out in disguised handwriting and had some 'appropriate' spelling mistakes! Benjamin was completely fooled and together with some other more sophisticated verses he had received, read out Augusta's, which ended …

> *And I hop a young Misus will soon be to com*
> *For indeed, here and there we here a strong hum*
> *That such a thing's going to be*
> *And weel be most happy and constantly crakky*
> *When we your intentions shall see.[93]*

It must have been obvious to all who knew them that there was an affectionate bond between Benjamin and Augusta, and much to the young couple's embarrassment, this was very heavily hinted at by Sir Charles Morgan[94] when, proposing the toast, he said that there was 'an event likely soon to take place when the young lady on the left side of the table would take the name of the worthy host'.

Very soon afterwards, on the 4th December, Benjamin and Augusta were married. Augusta said, many years later, that it was 'a boy and girl romance'. It was a romance that lasted for over forty years.

92   Benjamin Hall II, of Abercarn and Hensol, MP
93   *NLWJ vol. XII, no. 3, Summer 1962*, 'Benjamin Hall's Youth', Maxwell Fraser
94   Sir Charles Morgan, Bart., 1760–1846, father of the 1st Lord Tredegar

Chapter 2
Mr and Mrs Benjamin Hall
(1823-1838)

Mrs. Hall, a violent Welshwoman (which I like her for), maintained that the Welsh were in themselves 'excellent, simple good people'.[1]

Mrs. Hall rises daily in my estimation – there is in her a sincerity, and warmth of heart that is quite cynesol.[2]

The evening before the wedding was one of music and dancing. Augusta was young and very much in love and wanted everyone to be as happy as she was and to enjoy the festivities. The 'Caerphilly Harpist'[3] accompanied the dancing and the evening ended with everyone in good spirits.

There was one incident, however, which upset Mrs Waddington's carefully made plans. The wedding had been arranged to take place at Llanover Church at 11 o'clock on the morning of the 4th December 1823. On the day before, old Dr Hall,[4] Benjamin's grandfather, who was to conduct the ceremony, had arrived at Llanover and inexplicably declared that the ceremony must take place at 10 o'clock. No amount of pleading and cajoling could persuade the obstinate old man to change his mind. Fortunately, some of the guests were staying at Llanover and one of them, Augusta's cousin Frederick Waddington,[5] offered to hurry to Llanarth to advise the Misses Jones,[6] Augusta's bridesmaids, of the earlier time. The other bridesmaid was Benjamin's only sister Charlotte[7] who was already at Llanover. There was concern that Mrs Hawkins,[8] Benjamin's mother, could not be informed in time, but Dr Hall was adamant.

The morning of the wedding arrived and Augusta, dressed in white satin

---

1   Lady Louisa Stuart 1757–1851, youngest daughter of John, 3rd Earl of Bute, *NLWJ vol. XIII, no. 1, Summer 1963*, 'Young Mr and Mrs Hall 1823–30', Maxwell Fraser

2   Angharad Llwyd 1780–1886, *[T]ransactions of the [H]onourable [S]ociety of [C]ymmrodorion Session 1968, Part II*, 'Lady Llanover and Her Circle', Maxwell Fraser

3   It is not known which harpist this was.

4   Rev. Benjamin Hall DD, 1742–1825, Chancellor of the Diocese of Llandaff, Glamorganshire.

5   Frederick Waddington, 1803–? son of William Waddington, 1751–1818

6   Jane Mary, 1801–80 and Apollonia, 1804–90

7   Charlotte Hall, 1806–85

8   Benjamin Hall III's mother married Samuel Hawkins of Court Herbert, Glamorgan, in 1821

and silk, her blue eyes shining, looked her most beautiful. Dr Hall was eager to begin and he thought that as he and the bride and groom were there, there was no need to wait for the bridesmaids and guests! At the very last minute the Joneses of Llanarth appeared, and to everyone's immense relief Mrs Hawkins arrived just in time to join the procession. Other guests, unable to be warned of the earlier time, missed the ceremony.

The rest of the day seems to have passed without incident, the harpist playing all day while the guests partook of 'an elegant cold collation' in the middle of which stood a large wedding cake. The tenants were treated to a hot dinner.

The young couple set off in the early afternoon, only to return within the hour – a large piece of luggage had been left behind! There was much laughter and teasing as the missing piece was retrieved, then off they went once more to spend a few days at Trecastle.[9]

That evening the younger guests attended the Assembly in Abergavenny where Mr Bailey, High Sheriff for Monmouthshire, acted as Manager for the evening in the understandable absence of young Benjamin who had originally been named Manager. Such a good time was had by all that it was five o'clock the next morning before they returned to Llanover. Those remaining at Llanover watched the tenants and servants enjoying themselves dancing in the hall. Augusta's fervent wish, that everyone should be happy and joyful on her wedding day, seems to have been fulfilled.

Benjamin and Augusta must have presented a striking picture. He was very tall – some say 6ft 7ins – with a fine figure 'shown to the best advantage by the costume of that era';[10] she was small, dainty and very feminine. Benjamin was rather reserved, although amiable and kind, while Augusta was outgoing and vivacious with a very strong and determined character. Despite these differences they had much in common besides their obvious devotion to each other. In contrast to many members of the ruling classes of the time both were very conscious of the responsibilities that came with their wealth and position and had a genuine wish to improve the lives of their tenants and servants. They were always appreciative of any service performed by their domestic staff, no matter how small; they shared a sense of humour and a liking for music and dancing and, most significant for Wales, a determination

9   Trecastle is situated on the A40 trunk road between Brecon and Llandovery.
10 *NLWJ Vol. XIII no. 1 Summer 1963* 'Young Mr and Mrs Hall, 1823–1830', Maxwell Fraser

to support the Welsh language and culture.

By Christmas the newly wedded couple were established in their rented house in Hereford-shire.[11] There they were neighbours of Lady Greenly, which must have pleased Augusta as they no doubt continued to share their enthusiasm for all things connected with Wales. The Halls were very popular and friends and family visited them fre-quently. They returned the visits and were invited to stay with their new neighbours. They attended the church at Almeley and held Sunday evening services at Newport House, led by Benjamin. There were musical evenings when Benjamin would sing to Augusta's accompaniment. Benjamin had 'a superb voice' and Augusta was 'a delightful performer on the piano or harp', but was no singer![12]

Mrs Hall, later Lady Llanover

Image reproduced by kind permission of Gwent Archives

Their first child was born on 12th September 1824. Augusta went back to Llanover for the birth and the new baby was baptised there on the 3rd Octo-ber. She was named Augusta Charlotte Elizabeth, and the family's good friend Lady Greenly was one of her godmothers.[13]

Following their return to Newport House, life continued as before with musical entertainments and dancing, picnics and shooting parties, and great house parties on the anniversary of their wedding.

The old man who had almost ruined their wedding day, Benjamin's grand-father Dr Hall, died in February 1825. He had been his usual self when he and his granddaughter Charlotte visited Benjamin and Augusta at the end of the previous year and in spite of his age his sudden death came as a shock to the family. His memorial inscription at Llandaff reads:

Benjamin Hall, D.D., Precentor of this Church and Chancellor of the diocese; ob. 25 Feb. 1825 aet 83

"Ni bydd marw yn dragywydd" [He shall not die for ever]

---

11 Newport House, nr. Almeley

12 *NLWJ Vol. XIII no. 1 Summer 1963* 'Young Mr and Mrs Hall, 1823–1830', Maxwell Fraser

13 ibid

Almost a year later, on 9th January 1826, a new member of the Hall family made his appearance. Mr and Mrs Hall's son and heir was born at Newport House and this time Mrs Waddington went to Herefordshire to be with her daughter for the birth. The baby was baptised at Almeley[14] and was named Benjamin Hanbury Stuart.

In that same year Benjamin Hall was appointed High Sheriff of Monmouthshire and maybe that was the reason the young family left Newport House and returned to live at Abercarn. Benjamin's father had died in 1817 and under the terms of his will his widow had been left the Abercarn mansion for the remainder of her life, but it seems that she, now Mrs Hawkins, moved to Hampshire about 1826/7, and then to Brighton where, in 1839, she died.

Because Benjamin had not reached his majority when his father died the estate was left in the hands of trustees who managed it very well. However, as soon as he came of age, Benjamin began to organise his affairs in his own way. Properties such as the Rhymney estate and Hensol Castle were sold but for some reason the property at Pontypridd was retained. Gradually most of his properties were consolidated into a more manageable unit.

It is thought that the first eisteddfod that Augusta Hall attended was the Brecon Eisteddfod of 1826, held by the Cambrian Society of Gwent[15] under the patronage of Lord Rodney.[16] Among those who addressed the assembled crowd were the Rev. John Blackwell,[17] Colonel Wood and Sir Charles Morgan;[18] but it was the fine oratory of the Rev. Thomas Price, *Carnhuanawc*[19] that made the greatest impression on Mrs Hall. The enthusiastic young woman took his inspiring words extolling the virtues of the Welsh language to heart and the two became firm friends, working together for the good of the people and the country they both loved, to the end of his life.

This meeting, however, became to him ever afterwards peculiarly memorable, as an æra alike auspicious to Cambria's welfare, and gratifying to his personal feelings; for his honest and fervid eloquence proved the means of stimulating the inherent patriotism of Gwenynen Gwent [Lady Llanover], and gained for

---

14 His birth and baptism at Almeley were recorded in the Llanover Parish Records on 23rd October

15 The Cambrian Society of Gwent comprised the eastern counties of South Wales. Their first eisteddfod was held in Brecon in September 1822 and according to Edwin Poole in his *History of Brecknockshire* 'no one single gathering has since eclipsed [it].'

16 George Rodney, 3rd Baron Rodney, 1782-1842

17 Rev. John Blackwell, *Alun*, 1797-1841

18 Sir Charles Morgan, Bart., 1760–1846

19 The Rev. Thomas Price, 1787–1848, s/o Rev. Rice Price and his wife Mary (née Bowen). Vicar of Cwmdu from 1825 until his death in 1848

him the lifelong friendship of the Llanover families.[20]

THE REV. T. PRICE.

Rev. Thomas Price Carnhuanawc
Illustrated London News: Photograph John Weedy

By 1826 *Carnhuanawc* was already well known for his oratory, having spoken at several previous eisteddfodau. Young Mrs Hall had met a man whose zeal and love of Wales more than matched her own.

Thomas Price was a Welsh speaker from birth. He wrote in one of his small notebooks:

I have always spoken the Welsh from my infancy ... I suppose that the Welsh has been spoken by my ancestors, as their native tongue, ever since the dispersal of Babel. My father spoke it, my mother, and my grandfathers &c. &c.[21]

He attended the Grammar School[22] at Brecon from 1805 to 1811, in which year he was ordained. He was a man of many talents with wide ranging interests. He was a historian, a linguist and a Celtic scholar; also, through watching others and then practising in his own workshop, he had acquired some skill as a craftsman. He liked to make musical instruments, his first being a sort of lyre.

He took habitual delight in executing works of manual skill, and kept a carpenter's bench and chest of tools in constant use ... Thus early did he manifest at once his ingenuity and his ingenuousness, while framing a rude imitation of that graceful national instrument [the harp], which proved to be through life the favourite idol of his fancy.[23]

---

20 *The Literary Remains of the Rev. Thomas Price, Carnhuanawc*, ed. Jane Williams (Ysgafell)
21 ibid
22 Now Christ College
23 *The Literary Remains of the Rev. Thomas Price, Carnhuanawc*, ed. Jane Williams (Ysgafell)

His first recollection of the harp was the single-stringed harp of 'old Sam[24] the harper' who lived at Builth, and whom he had 'often seen, previous to the year 1800, going towards Llanafan feast and other places', and during his time in Brecon young Thomas had harp lessons from David Watkins[25] of Llanfaes.

The first thing he taught me was to place my fingers on the strings to make the four chord notes of the octave, viz. G B D G, placing the three fingers and thumb on those strings, leaving a string untouched between each finger, and two strings between the fore finger and thumb ...

He was very particular in making me keep my hand in a proper position ... and when I forgot this position of the hand, the old fellow would take hold of my thumb and screw it upwards most viciously, at the same time pulling my fore finger down in the opposite direction, accompanying this gentle practical admonition with a spiteful sounding ee–ee &c.[26]

Carnhuanawc's writings appeared in various Welsh language publications and he also wrote considerable works in English.

In 1823 the Welsh Literary Society of Brecon was formed 'by the exertion of his indefatigable diligence and zeal' and he was elected its first president. Not long afterwards, on 24th November 1824 a meeting was held 'of Gentlemen interested in the Encouragement of Welsh Music'. Again, Thomas Price was involved and the Breconshire Society for Welsh Minstrelsy was formed 'for the encouragement of performers on the Welsh Harp, and the Instruction of Poor Blind Boys on that Instrument.'

[Thomas Price] obtained a sufficient number of annual subscribers to remunerate Mr. John Jones[27] for instructing, at Brecon, a certain number of blind youths to play upon the national instrument, and also to provide triple harps for the pupils.[28]

John Jones was already well known as a skilful player on the old instrument. He was born in 1800 in a gypsy tent at the side of the road to

---

24 Sam Davies (Hen Sam). He played a small single-stringed harp and accompanied dancing in the open air and played his harp while walking. *Telyn a Thelynor*, Ann Rosser

25 David Watkins, Llanfaes. He played the single-stringed harp and had a special way of changing its sound by means of *gwrachod,* angular pegs made of thorn twigs, for when he accompanied dancing

26 *The Literary Remains of the Rev. Thomas Price, Carnhuanawc*, ed. Jane Williams (Ysgafell)

27 John Wood Jones, 1800–1844

28 *The Literary Remains of the Rev. Thomas Price, Carnhuanawc*, ed. Jane Williams (Ysgafell)

Dolgellau,[29] a member of the famous Wood[30] family of harpers and fiddlers.

Although it is likely that Augusta was familiar with the harp – she was a player of some proficiency and is said to have had lessons with Elias Parish-Alvars[31] – maybe the 1826 eisteddfod was where she first heard the *triple* harp being played.

Elias Parish Alvars

John Jones
The Literary Remains of Rev. Thomas Price
Illustration by Lady Llanover

The contest for the Silver Harp then took place, which was gained by Mr. John Jones, Harper to the Breconshire Minstrelsy Society, who acquitted himself with his usual well known talent. He was invested with the Silver Harp by Lady Rodney, amidst the universal applause of the assembly.[32]

The concert on the Tuesday evening was very well attended and 'the whole of the performance went off with the utmost

29 *Cymru* 1908 – Hen Gerddorion Dolgellau

30 The most well known gypsy family in Wales, beginning with Abraham Wood, c. 1699–1799, a fiddle player, *The Story of the Harp in Wales*, Osian Ellis

31 Elias Parish, 1808-1849, *Arglwyddes Llanofer*, Rachel Ley, p. 69. He took the name Parish–Alvars when he became famous

32 *The Cambrian*

éclat.' The conductor was Mr John Parry,[33] *Bardd Alaw*, 'the distinguished editor of the *Welsh Melodies'* who had arranged for the 'first talent in the land' to entertain the audience. Braham,[34] the renowned tenor, was in fine voice and Lindley[35] accompanied him on the 'violoncello'. There were other vocalists who charmed the audience, and instrumentalists, amongst whom were the violinist Mori[36] and the flautist Nicholson who gave 'masterly performances.' The attendance at the Church for the Oratorio was also good, and the concert on the Wednesday night was a great success.

Before leaving Brecon, the performers asked Mr Parry to express their thanks to Mr Vaughan, the secretary, for his courteous attention and the President asked him to 'convey his thanks to the Professional Ladies and Gentlemen, and to assure them that they had charmed and delighted everybody by their eminent performances during the Festival.'

It is but due to Mr. Parry to say, that although he has conducted so many of these Musical Festivals in the Principality with such satisfaction to all who have attended, his services have hitherto been the free and gratuitous offerings of his patriotism.[37]

It was about this time that Benjamin Hall began negotiations to buy the manor of Park Lettice, which had once been a part of the manor of Llanover. Mr Waddington had tried to buy the manor when he and his family first came to Llanover; Benjamin succeeded where his father-in-law had failed.

The young Hall family soon moved house once more. Early in 1828 Augusta's father died suddenly[38] when staying with them at Abercarn. Because of Mrs Waddington's delicate health, her husband had decided she would be better off staying at home in Llanover rather than making the short journey to Abercarn in the very cold weather, so he made the journey alone. He was still an active man and one morning shortly after his arrival he took a walk in the frosty, snow-covered countryside. That night he went to bed at his usual early time. The following morning his valet found him on the floor in a coma. A doctor was summoned immediately and a chaise was sent to bring Mrs Waddington to her husband. The poor man died later that day without

---

33   John Parry, *Bardd Alaw*, 1776-1851
34   John Braham, (real name Abraham), b. London of Jewish parents, 20/3/1777, d. London 17/2/1856
35   Robert Lindley, b. Rotherham, 4/3/1776. d. London, 13/6/1855. English 'cellist and composer
36   Nicholas Mori, 1796/7- 1839, English violinist and music publisher of Italian descent
37   *The Cambrian*
38   Benjamin Waddington died 11th January 1828

regaining consciousness, his wife, daughter and son-in-law at his side. In spite of reassurances that it had been at his insistence that she had stayed at home, Mrs Waddington felt very deeply that she should not have allowed him to go to Abercarn without her. Her daughter Frances, shocked at hearing the news and distressed that her mother should blame herself, wrote to her, saying:

> ... *you were, and had been, the sole pleasure of his life, the sole occupation, the sole subject matter that mixed with his thoughts and plans ... you made all his happiness ... he did not anticipate his end was so near.*

The funeral at Llanover was a very moving occasion with more than four hundred local people present, all 'as still as death'. In a letter to Lady Greenly shortly afterwards, Mrs Waddington wrote:

> *I think no person was ever followed to the grave by more sincere mourners. He had not an enemy in the world and his charities were so numerous, he has benefited so many, that blessings have followed him ...* [39]

When preparing his will Mr Waddington had taken great care to provide properly and fairly for his family. As it was unlikely that Frances would ever return to live in Monmouthshire, and as Augusta was so passionate about Llanover, he had come to an agreement with Frances and her husband that Augusta should inherit Llanover, while Frances would be compensated financially from the estate. Mrs Waddington, widowed at the age of fifty-six, was to have the tenancy of *Tŷ Uchaf* for the rest of her life.

Loving Llanover as she did, and anxious to comfort her grieving mother and care for her during her spells of ill health, Augusta thought that they should go to live in *Tŷ Uchaf*. Her devoted husband, always wanting his wife's happiness, agreed and so Augusta returned to her much-loved birthplace, the Abercarn mansion from then on being used as a 'holiday home'.

Benjamin and Augusta, both enthusiastic about all things Welsh, shared a dream – to build a house which would become a focus for Welsh culture, a centre for bards, musicians, historians and academics to meet, where they could study, exchange views and enjoy the society of like minded people. The construction of *Llys Llanofer* began in 1828 on the Park Lettice / Llanover border, the work being undertaken by Thomas Hopper. [40] Benjamin Hall, having excellent taste and an aptitude for architecture, insisted on a simple design

---

39 *NLWJ Vol. XIII no. 1 Summer 1963* 'Young Mr and Mrs Hall, 1823–1830', Maxwell Fraser
40 Thomas Hopper, (1776–1856), a favourite of King George IV

and although it has been described as a 'vast Gothic monstrosity', photographs show the mansion to have been an elegant building 'in a plain, dignified Jacobean style'.[41]

In November 1829, during one of the coldest winters in living memory, the young Hall family and Mrs Waddington went to Rome to visit Frances, Augusta's sister, and her family. Poor Mrs Waddington, never robust, felt the cold se verely. The wintry weather took the local people by surprise and when it snowed the Bun-

Llys Llanofer-Llanover House

sen children were delighted by the rare occurrence. Christmas was celebrated according to the custom begun by Charles Bunsen when he and Frances were first married; he reproduced the family Christmases he had so loved as a child[42] and the whole family enjoyed a very festive time.

In the late spring Benjamin was called back to London. There was much discussion as to whether or not he should leave as Augusta was pregnant, and it would have been very unwise for her to travel back with him just then. Eventually he decided to go, knowing that his wife would be cared for by her family. A baby boy was born on the 2nd June 1830 and was named Benjamin Caradoc Trevor Francis Zacchia.

There had been no mail between England and Italy due to the troubles in France, and no doubt anxious about her husband Augusta and her party set off on their journey home in July, knowing nothing of the revolution in France. They were travelling in their own coaches and in Lyons their coat of arms was mistaken for that of the French King. Their courier was arrested and it was only due to the doughty Augusta's intervention that they were proved to be innocent of any involvement in the troubles. The courier was eventually released and they were able to continue their journey, but Mrs

---

41   *NLWJ Vol. XIII no. 1 Summer 1963* 'Young Mr and Mrs Hall, 1823–1830', Maxwell Fraser
42   ibid

Waddington's nerves were badly shaken. It was a very uncomfortable journey and due to the heat they travelled by night, with the poor baby unable to bear clothes on his hot little body.

In the meantime Benjamin, worried about the lack of news from his young family, set off to try to find them. He hurried back to France knowing only that they intended to return through Lyons. By a stroke of good fortune they met a few miles from Boulogne – one can only imagine their relief at being together again, and Benjamin's joy at seeing his new son for the first time.[43]

They must all have been very thankful to arrive safely back in London where they stayed for some time. Mrs Waddington received invitations to visit friends from her youth, Princess Elizabeth, by then the wife of the Landgrave of Hesse-Homburg, and Princess Mary, the wife of the Duke of Gloucester. At the time, she was not well enough to accept either invitation but later recovered sufficiently to visit the Duchess who had thoughtfully arranged to receive her ailing friend on the ground floor to save her having to climb the stairs. Young Augusta Charlotte Elizabeth accompanied her and the little girl made her grandmother very proud when she charmed the Duchess with her good manners.

They all returned to Llanover in 1831, the year that Benjamin Hall was elected Member of Parliament for the Monmouthshire Boroughs.[44] The election took place in early May and Benjamin won by a small majority over his opponent, the Marquis of Worcester.[45] The Marquis, who had held the seat since 1813, was naturally very upset at his defeat and sought the advice of his friend Sir Charles Morgan.

The Newport Town Clerk at the time was Thomas Prothero, who had been agent to Sir Charles for twenty-five years. He was a devious man who enjoyed a grand lifestyle and he was frequently accused of corruption. Disliked and feared throughout the county, he realised that his connection with Sir Charles could count against him if more direct action should develop from the present unrest in the labouring classes.[46] He cut all his ties with his former employer and gave his support to Benjamin Hall.

Sir Charles by this time thoroughly disliked Prothero and arranged to have the vote in Newport checked. It became clear that some of the burgesses had

43   *NLWJ Vol. XIII no. 1 Summer 1963* 'Young Mr and Mrs Hall, 1823–1830', Maxwell Fraser
44   Monmouth, Newport and Usk
45   Henry Somerset, Marquis of Worcester, 1792–1853
46   Merthyr rising of 1831

not been entitled to vote and the Marquis, on receiving this information, petitioned Parliament to have the vote overturned. A House of Commons committee met in July, and having heard counsel for both sides, resolved:

> *That Benjamin Hall Esq. is not duly elected, and ought not to have been re-turned to serve in this present Parliament for the town and borough of Mon-mouth. That the Rt. Hon. Henry Somerset, commonly called Marquis of Worcester, is duly elected and will serve as member for the said borough.*[47]

There is no suggestion that Benjamin Hall was involved in any deception. It seems that Prothero acted on his own, to ingratiate himself with Mr Hall, and he was very fortunate that no further investigation took place into how ineligible people had been allowed to vote![48]

By July 1831 Benjamin was no longer a Member of Parliament. However, at the next election in December 1832 he was genuinely elected to serve the Monmouthshire Boroughs, and held the seat in the election in January 1835.

Towards the end of 1832 Mrs Waddington and Augusta heard some very disturbing news concerning Augusta's cousin Anne Stratton (née D'Ewes).[49] Anne's husband, George Frederick Stratton,[50] had appeared to be a suitable match for Anne, but he had squandered not only all his own money, but also his wife's, and even his elderly mother's money. The scoundrel, facing ruin, had run away to America leaving the two unfortunate women with nothing. The house, Park Hall and all its contents were to be sold! Anne had been left Mrs Delany's collection of paintings and flower mosaics, so when the news reached Llanover Mrs Waddington became very upset at the thought of those unique works of art, Mrs Delany's flower mosaics, being sold to the highest bidder and ending up who knows where!

Realising how upset his wife and his mother-in-law were, Benjamin went to the sale, determined to keep these works of art in the family.

> *The bidding was so brisk that Benjamin almost gave up the contest, but … he overheard a Dealer say 'he could make a great deal of money by shewing them at the West End of Town'.*[51]

That was all Benjamin needed! The very thought of those precious works

---

47 *Monmouthshire Merlin*

48 *Newport First Stop – 100 Years of News Stories,* Derrick Cyril Vaughan

49 Anne D'Ewes, 1778-1861, daughter of Bernard D'Ewes and his wife Anne De La Bere

50 George Frederick Stratton of Tew Park, Gloucestershire, later of Park Hall. m. Anne D'Ewes in 1805

51 *NLWJ XIII* 'Benjamin and Augusta Hall 1831-36', Maxwell Fraser

being the subject of a public exhibition was enough to spur him on! He eventually outbid all the others and the flower mosaics were his for 300 guineas.

About this time a Breton writer and art critic, Alexis Rio,[52] was travelling in the United Kingdom and he came to Llanover with a letter of introduction from Augusta's sister Frances Bunsen.[53]

> ... *he glories in being a* **Breton**, *in having spoken all the years of his childhood exclusively the Breton language, but as this is preserved in Bretagne in much less perfection than the Welsh in Wales, he makes it the principal object of a journey to Great Britain to study his native language at its source.*[54]

Rio was warmly welcomed at Llanover and particularly enjoyed the company of *Carnhuanawc* who had travelled in Brittany a few years previously and was able to converse with the young Breton in his own language. *Carnhuanawc* came to hold M. Rio in high esteem thinking of him as 'an extraordinary genius'.

On one occasion, *[Carnhuanawc]* took a pen, and drawing a zig-zag stroke, said, 'That is Rio, he was a complete flash of lighting,' meaning that he had astonished and illuminated in the most eccentric and unexpected manner.[55]

The Joneses at Llanarth also made Rio welcome, where, being an ardent Roman Catholic, he was possibly more at ease. The daughter of his hosts, Apollonia Jones[56] was a charming young woman and in February 1834 she and M. Rio were married.

One of Rio's reasons for coming to Wales was to study the Welsh language and compare it with his own language, which was under threat from French oppression.

> *Mr. Price had a great regard for Monsieur Rio (Riew), the Breton, both on account of his own brilliant talents, and from sympathies of various kinds.*

Towards the end of 1833 *Carnhuanawc* received an invitation to attend a meeting in Abergavenny, organised by some of the townsmen in order to establish a new society.

> *On Friday, the 22nd November, 1833, the Cymdeithas Cymreigyddion y Fenni, or Welsh Literary Society of Abergavenny, was formed by five and twenty re-*

---

52 Alexis Francois Rio (or Rieuw), 1797–1874, born on the Island of Arz, Morbihan, Brittany
53 *NLWJ Vol. XI No. 4 Winter 1960* 'The Waddingtons of Llanover', Maxwell Fraser
54 *NLWJ XIII* 'Benjamin and Augusta Hall 1831-36', Maxwell Fraser
55 *The Literary Remains of the Rev. Thomas Price, Carnhuanawc*, ed. Jane Williams (Ysgafell)
56 Apollonia Jones, 1804-1890, daughter of John Jones and his wife Mary, née Lee

spectable and zealous Welshmen of the town and neighbourhood, who assembled at the Sun Inn... [57]

The Rev. John Evans, vicar of Llanover, was appointed President; Mr Thomas Bevan,[58] Llanwenarth, Secretary; Mr T.E.Watkins,[59] of Blaenavon, Bard; and the Rev. Thomas Price, *Carnhuanawc*, Correspondent. The motto adopted by the Society was 'Oes y Byd i'r Iaith Gymraeg'.[60] Twenty-six members were enrolled and Thomas Price, although not able to be present, was placed first on the list as a mark of respect. In his letter apologising for his unavoidable absence he wrote, in Welsh, about what he would have said had he been there, namely, the importance of teaching Welsh to children in the day schools as well as Sunday schools, and of persuading Welsh parents to give Cambrian names to their children 'instead of adopting foreign ones now in common use ...'[61]

Five days later another meeting was held to agree the rules of the Society and to elect a committee. Another fourteen members were enrolled and 'the literary objects of the union were prosecuted with ardour, intelligence, and research.' Three more meetings took place in December, two in January 1834 and two in February, 'all of them full of spirit, eloquence and poetry.' Within three months, membership had grown to seventy-five, the majority of whom were from the 'lower classes'. The President, as he was vicar of Llanover, was asked to approach Mr and Mrs Hall regarding their support, and they were among the first of the 'upper class of society' to become members, as were Lady Greenly, Sir Charles Morgan of Tredegar, Mr John Guest[62] and Lady Charlotte Guest.[63] Alexis Rio was also one of the early members and this was the start of the strong link that was forged between the Abergavenny Cymreigyddion Society and Brittany.[64]

Mr. Price soon afterwards addressed to the committee a letter which evinced his anxious desire for the moral welfare of the Society's members, by protesting against a proposed rule which would have authorized expenditure for

---

57 *The Literary Remains of the Rev. Thomas Price, Carnhuanawc*, ed. Jane Williams
58 Thomas Bevan, *Caradawc y Fenni*, 1802-1882
59 Thomas Evan Watkins, *Eiddil Ifor*, 1801-1889
60 The duration of the world to the Welsh Language. *The Literary Remains of the Rev. Thomas Price, Carnhuanawc*, ed. Jane Williams
61 *The Literary Remains of the Rev. Thomas Price, Carnhuanawc*, ed. Jane Williams
62 Josiah John Guest, 1785–1852. Created a baronet in 1838
63 Lady Charlotte Elizabeth Guest (née Bertie, later Schreiber), 1812–1895
64 *NLWJ Vol. XI No. 4* 'Winter 1960 The Waddingtons of Llanover', Maxwell Fraser

refreshments.[65]

In March the same year it was announced that the Gwent and Dyfed Royal Eisteddfod and Music Festival would be held in Cardiff on the 20th, 21st and 22nd of August 'under the special patronage of their Royal Highnesses the Duchess of Kent and the Princess Victoria'. The president was to be the Marquis of Bute and the conductor Mr John Parry, *Bardd Alaw*. There were to be prizes for poems and essays written in Welsh and in English, one of which was for an essay on "The Advantages resulting from the preservation of the Welsh Language, and National Costumes[66] of Wales".

On the first day of the great event the President, the Marquis of Bute, headed the opening procession from the Town Hall to the Castle. He was followed by the Vice-Presidents, Sir Charles Morgan, and Sir John Nicholl, then the judges of the competitions, the officers of the committee and several members of Parliament, the last of these mentioned in the newspaper report being Benjamin Hall!

Much has been made of the fact that the Duchess of Kent and Princess Victoria were present at this Eisteddfod, but the report of the Eisteddfod in *The Cambrian* states:

If there were a single cause for regret on an occasion so well calculated to awaken national and local prejudices, it was that the distinguished Patronesses of such a festival – their Royal Highnesses the Duchess of Kent and the Princess Victoria – were not present. The fact of their probable absence was, however, so well known, that the disappointment thence arising was materially diminished, and we trust, as the event had proved, without any serious detriment to the undertaking.

The prize for the essay on the subject of the Welsh Language and National Costumes of Wales, which was 'a seal ring, with a Welsh Motto engraved on a Welsh Pebble, value £10. 10s', had been offered by the *Gwyneddigesau* [ladies of Gwynedd]. There were entries from Mrs Hall and Lady Greenly, and one other which arrived too late to be judged.

This essay was written by the Rev. J. Blackwell who was already well known in eisteddfodic circles. Lady Greenly's pseudonym was 'Llwydlaes' and her entry was complimented for its style and language; but it was Augusta Hall who won, signing herself *Gwenynen Gwent* [the Bee of Gwent], the

---

65   *The Literary Remains of the Rev. Thomas Price, Carnhuanawc*, ed. Jane Williams
66   Note the plural 'Costumes'

name by which she came to be known throughout Wales. The Marquis of Bute 'claimed the privilege and presented the ring to Mrs Hall, of Llanover, Monmouthshire, the fair and successful Candidate.'[67] Fortunately Lady Greenly's unassuming and generous nature enabled her to write:

> ...*Mrs. Hall was called up to receive the Ring from Lord Bute amidst a **thunder** of applause – she had kept the secret so profoundly that everybody was as much surprised as pleased, and I hope that even I (Llwydlaes) did not envy her success **too much**...*

In another letter, a week later, she quotes 'dear Mrs. Waddington', saying:

> ... *[she] told me **I** ought to have had the Ring, for I had no one to assist me in writing the essay, ... I could not agree, Mrs. Hall took great pains and had opportunities of research which I had not, and deserves a reward for her diligence.*[68]

About this time a series of watercolour pictures, representing the costumes of parts of Wales, were produced. They were dedicated to 'the nobility and gentry of Wales' and have been attributed to Augusta Hall. They were said to have been entered as illustrations for her essay, but a recent study[69] of these pictures has thrown doubt upon these assumptions. Some of the watercolours are signed *A. Cadwalader / Cadwallader* while others are unsigned. While no record has been found of an A. Cadwallader, it is interesting to note that a Bridget Cadwaladr[70] spent many years in London in the service of Lord and Lady Llanover.

Gwent Costume
Image reproduced by kind permission of Monmouthshire County Council, Abergavenny Museum

---

67 *The Cambrian.*

68 In a letter to Louisa Hastings (née Lowe), d/o Humphrey Lowe of Bromsgrove, Worcs. She married Capt, later Admiral Sir Thomas Hastings in 1827

69 *NLWJ Vol. XXXIV No. 2, 2007,* 'Lady Llanover and the Welsh Costume Prints', Michael Freeman

70 Bridget *(Dafydd)* Cadwaladr, daughter of Dafydd Cadwaladr and sister of Betsy Cadwaladr *(Elizabeth Davis, Balaclava nurse),* died 1878 and is buried in the graveyard of Capel Ed, Goetre

In the National Library of Wales there is an album[71] of these watercolours, entitled *National Costumes of Wales*, which was bound by 'E. Rees and Son, Book sellers and C. Abergavenny'. This album is thought to have been owned by Lady Llanover, and it is known that she had a 'Book of Welsh Costumes'.

Many of the younger people were 'very correctly dressed from Mrs Hall's "Book of Welsh Costumes"', and looked extremely well.[72]

Another album in the National Library has the handwritten inscription inside, 'Frances Jane Blackwell, September, 1837'.[73]

The Rev. Blackwell's essay[74] gives detailed descriptions of the costumes of parts of Wales, including the details of clothes worn by men in the tenth century, referring to an illustration in a manuscript copy of The Laws of Howel Dda. Differences in the dress worn by the women of Anglesey, Dyfed and Gwent are commented on, and he could see no reason why the mode of dress adopted by our ancestors due to the climate should not still be suitable in 1834.

Gwenynen Gwent's essay also remarked on the suitability of the locally made fabrics for the Welsh way of life. She writes of the 'hale and robust' mothers and grandmothers 'secure from the storm, under the protection of the warm *woollen* gown, and comfortable cloak ... with a *neat* and *serviceable* beaver hat, and black *woollen* stockings' while the '*delicate* and *cotton clad daughter* or *grand-daughter*' shelters, shivering, under a hedge or tree 'with her flimsy straw bonnet, saturated with water, and dyed like a rainbow by the many coloured streams descending from its numerous and once gaudy ribbons'. This, Mrs Hall states, results from the 'absurd abandonment of ancient and wise habits'[75] and she exhorted those with any influence to set an example.

It is interesting to contemplate what would have been the effect on Mrs Hall had the Rev. Blackwell's work been received in time to be adjudicated, and *he* declared the winner!

Would *Gwenynen Gwent* have been as zealous in her fight to retain and restore all that she loved about Wales? Would she have become as well known

71 NLW Album 299
72 *NLWJ Vol. XXXIV No. 2, 2007*, 'Lady Llanover and the Welsh Costume Prints', Michael Freeman
73 I am grateful to Michael Freeman, Ceredigion Museum, for information re Welsh Costumes
74 *Beauties of Alun*, J. Clarke, Ruthin; H. Hughes, London, 1851, and *Cambrian Journal*, 1861
75 Essay on the *Advantages Resulting from the Preservation of the Welsh Language and National Costumes of Wales*, by Mrs Hall of Llanover, Cardiff 1834

throughout the Principality for her enthusiastic support for everything Welsh?

Returning to Cardiff, and the Eisteddfod - on the Thursday the President remarked that

> ... *as this was the birth-day of our gracious King William the Fourth, he considered that their proceedings could not more appropriately commence than by the recitation of an Ode composed in honour of his Majesty by an eminent Bard, then present – (Tegid)*[76]

The Rev. John Jones, of Christ Church, Oxford, was then introduced by the Rev. W. B. Knight, and was received with general applause.[77] He then read his especially composed Welsh Ode 'with a fervour and energy which drew forth great applause.'

The previous day he had received the prize for the best Welsh Englyn to be inscribed on a mantelpiece in a gentleman's kitchen. The prize was a Drinking Horn mounted in silver, with a Welsh motto, but perhaps the greater prize was yet to come – this was the englyn that was later inscribed above the entrance to the servants' hall in the as yet incomplete Llys Llanover.

Englyn y Buelin

Gwastraff – eisieu; drwg ystryw, – gwarth a ddwg,
Ac wrth ddwyn gwarth, distryw;
Da i bawb cynildeb yw,
A thad i gyfoeth ydyw.[78]

The Drinking Horn

It is the cause of waste, want, trickery and shame;
Frugality is good for everyone
And is the creator of wealth.[79]

As still required at eisteddfodau today, competitors for the written competitions were asked to send their work 'in sealed packets, under feigned signatures, (the real Names sent sealed up)'. This led to an amusing incident when *Drew-bach* [Little Wren] was called upon to present himself. He did not come forward at the time but the reporter noted that 'Little Wren some time after presented himself, when he appeared about sixteen stone weight!!!'[80]

---

76   Rev. John Jones, *Tegid*, 1792-1852
77   *The Cambrian*
78   *Cymru*, 1908/9 'Gwenynen Gwent', L.M. Owen
79   I am grateful to Delyth Clark for this translation and to Mrs Olwen Jones for arranging it
80   *The Cambrian*

There were several competitions for the harp.

1. A Miniature Silver Harp, of the value of £5 5s. with a Gratuity at the discretion of the Committee towards Travelling Expenses, to the best Proficient on the Single-stringed Harp without Pedals.

2. A Miniature Silver Harp, of the value of £5 5s. with a Gratuity at the discretion of the Committee towards Travelling Expenses, for the best Proficient on the Triple-stringed Harp.

3. A Medal or a Premium, value £3 3s. to the best Singer with the Harp, according to the manner of Gwent and Dyfed.

4. A Medal or a Premium, value £3 3s. to the best Singer of *Penillion* with the Harp according to the Northwalian manner.

A blind harper, Edward Watkins of Merthyr Tydfil, who played 'with a taste, pathos, and brilliancy, that called forth general approbation', won the first competition. One of the other competitors was John Jones[81] of Caerphilly, son of Edward Jones.[82] Because the competition required a 'Single-stringed Harp without Pedals' John had removed the pedals from the old instrument[83] especially for the competition. It was the harp his father had played for King George III when his Majesty visited Abergavenny.

The competition for the best player of the triple harp was won by Hugh Pugh[84] of Dolgellau. There were no other competitors but 'he afforded a masterly display of his skill on the instrument'. He was one of the most brilliant harpists to have been brought up in Dolgellau and had first come to the attention of the country as a harpist when he won the silver harp at the Bala Eisteddfod, about 1830.[85] He went to London where he played the harp before the royal family and moved in the best circles. Sadly he died in London at the early age of 29.

At this eisteddfod Mr Price was very impressed with a 'wonderful Welsh boy' called William Manuel, son of Thomas and Mary Manuel, natives of North Wales. Both parents were Welsh speakers and although existing on Mr Manuel's poor wage as a miner, they were a very respectable family.[86] Mary,

---

81 It is possible that he was the 'Caerphilly harper' who played at Benjamin and Augusta's wedding.

82 Edward Jones, 1768–1814, author of *The Caerphilly March*

83 Item No. 91.30, St Fagans: National History Museum

84 Hugh Pugh, of Dolgellau, 1811–1840. He died in London and is buried in Bunhill Fields

85 *Cymru*, 1908, 'Hen Gerddorion Dolgellau'

86 Thomas Manuel, wife Mary, 1804–1844; sons Freeman 1827–?, Thomas 1828–1851, William 1830–1842, Edward 1833–1837; daughters Catherine 1835–? and Elizabeth (later in Lady Llanover's service)

the daughter of a farmer, was very fond of reading and was fluent in both Welsh and English. She realised that her sons had an 'extraordinary thirst for learning' and taught herself to read and translate Latin and Greek in order to help them. The eldest son, Thomas, was an excellent scholar of Latin and Greek as well as Welsh and English, but William, the second son, proved to be even more scholarly, being able by the age of four to read all the languages mastered by Thomas, and also Hebrew. In a newspaper report of the time the correspondent states:

> The Rev. Gentleman[87] then proceeded to remark that he had himself examined this wonderful child, [William] and found him proficient in the Greek, Hebrew, and (the language which surpassed them all), in Welsh, which he could read, not only fluently, but upside down, or any sort of side.[88]

His comments were met with laughter from his listeners. The Rev. Knight concluded by saying 'there was only one way in which he could account for the prodigious attainments of the boy, and it was by saying, "see what Wales can do!"' – which brought cheers and laughter from the audience.

The youngest son, Edward, showed even more promise, being able to read English, Welsh, German, Latin, Greek and Hebrew at the age of four years. Sadly this remarkable child died before he reached his fifth birthday. William too died young; he was twelve years old and had had a 'most successful career' at Christ's Hospital.[89] Thomas reached 'early manhood' but died in 1851. All three boys died 'of a decline'.

The Manuels had an older son, Freeman Manuel, who went to Australia,[90] and two daughters, Elizabeth and Catherine.

Mrs Hall's success at the Cardiff Eisteddfod brought her an invitation to become a member of the Gorsedd. In her effusive letter of acceptance, dated London, October 5th, 1834, she wrote:

> Sir, May I express my gratitude to you and all the Bards who formed the recent Gorsedd for the honour of being elected as a member of the praiseworthy body to which you belong. I ask you to believe that the joy this honour brings me is as full as it was unexpected … I will always count this occasion of my reception into the number of the Bards as amongst the most blessed of my life and there

---

87　The Rev. William Bruce Knight, 1785-1845

88　*The Cambrian*

89　Christ College, Brecon.

90　Freeman Manuel was listed in the Electoral year 1856 in Victoria, South Melbourne

will not be seen in their ranks a more fervent supporter than Your Servant, Gwenynen Gwent[91]

At the time of writing Mrs Hall was in London preparing for a journey to the Continent. She was obviously delighted at becoming more closely involved with the culture of the country she loved, but her joy would have been somewhat diminished when, six months later in London, her little boy died.[92] He is buried in London.

John Jones, the harper, was invited to attend the second anniversary of the Abergavenny Cymreigyddion Society which was publicly celebrated by 'a meeting of the native Cymry [the Welsh people] and many distinguished visitors', with Mr John Guest as President. The harper was living in Clifton at this time, the Breconshire Society for Welsh Minstrelsy having been 'marred and broken up by the party politics of the borough.'

Jones voted at an election for Mr. Lloyd Watkins; the powerful family of Tredegar, its friends and retainers, retaliated by withdrawing their subscriptions from the society. Its ruin ensued, the poor blind pupils were dispersed, and the harper removed himself to Clifton.[93]

On the 2nd November John Jones wrote to Mr Bevan, secretary of the Society, thanking him for the 'preference' and saying that he could not charge under Five Pounds 'as traveling [sic] and other expences [sic] will be considerable'. He added:

I am also sorry to say that my best Harp met with an accident some time since the one which I now play on is not so good but such as it is I shall be happy to do my endeavour with.[94]

The meeting was held on 25th and 26th November 1835 at the Free Grammar School, and *Carnhuanawc* addressed the meeting on his favourite subjects with his usual flair and eloquence.

M. Rio should have been President at the following year's meeting, held once again at the Free Grammar School, on Wednesday 23rd and Thursday 24th November 1836, but he was not in the country at the time and W. Williams of Llandybie took the chair in his place. He asked Mr Hall to propose

---

91 A very rough translation from the original Welsh by the author.
92 Benjamin Caradoc Hall. b. Rome 1830. d. London 8th June1835
93 *The Literary Remains of the Rev. Thomas Price, Carnhuanawc*, ed. Jane Williams *(Ysgafell)*
94 NLW Ref. 13182-3E, letter dated 2nd Nov 1835

a toast at the dinner on the first day.[95]

In his address Mr Hall said that his expectations for the Society 'had been *far exceeded* by the fertile genius and the unwearied exertions of his countrymen', which brought cheers from his listeners. He paid tribute to 'the little band of patriotic Welshmen', those who, in the past, had travelled miles 'through many a stormy night to consider the best means of preserving a language which they prized, and promoting a literature which they had the good taste and right feeling to admire.'

On the second day Mr Hall again took the opportunity to speak to the meeting. He told of his delight at the first day's proceedings and his satisfaction at the healthy state of the Society's funds. Membership was increasing and all those present were 'animated by the same soul-thrilling spirit of nationality.' There was great cheering when he announced that he had very recently received the news that a Welsh *Metropolitan* newspaper was about to be published, its object being 'the diffusion of knowledge in Welsh,

A Bassett Jones Harp

Image reproduced by kind permission of
Cambridge Harp Association

Detail of a Bassett Jones Harp

Image reproduced by kind permission of Cambridge Harp Association

the perpetuation of the literature of Wales, and the maintenance of the best interests of Welshmen.' It was to be called *Y Cymro* [the Welshman] and would appear every fortnight, at 'the usual price of 4d.'

Mr Hall said he was well aware that the interest he

took in matters regarding the Welsh language caused people in certain quarters to express strongly their disapproval but he welcomed this criticism as he was certain that the more calm discussion there was on the subject 'the more clearly would the merits of their national efforts appear.'

That morning he had heard 'such delightful and sweet streams of melody'[96] that he decided to offer at the next anniversary not just one prize, as originally intended, but two; three guineas for the best female singer and two guineas for the second best.

He also proposed that part of the expenses of the bards and minstrels who had travelled some distance to be there should be met by subscriptions from the friends of the society. This suggestion met with the approval of the audience.

There followed yet another speech, in Welsh, by the eloquent and fervent *Carnhuanawc*, once more exhorting his listeners to 'cherish and cultivate their ancient language'. Then the 'venerable *Cawrdaf*',[97] co-judge with *Carnhuanawc*, came forward to award the prizes of the day. The winners of the various competitions were duly presented with their prizes and there was 'immense applause' when Miss Hall, *Y Wenynen Fach* [the Little Bee], invested the winner of 'the best poetical composition on the emphatic exclamation *King Arthur is not dead.'*[98] B. Bowen, *Meudwy Glan Taf*, was the winner of the medal, value 3 guineas.

Mrs Divett (née Ross) gave the prize of a 'new and handsome triple harp, of the best construction, built expressly for this occasion' by Bassett Jones of Cardiff.

THE NEW HARPS AT THE ABERGAVENNY EISTEDDFOD
We understand that these beautiful instruments were manufactured by Mr Bassett Jones, now residing at Cardiff. They reflect very great credit on his mechanical skill.[99]

The prize was awarded to Thomas Griffiths, Tredegar, and presented to him by Madame Rio[100] 'whose affability could not fail to enhance the value of the prize'. Another competitor, fifteen-year-old Susannah Prichard of Crickhowell, was praised for her 'pretty taste' and was said to have 'consid-

---

96 *The Silurian*
97 William Ellis Jones, *Cawrdaf*, 1795-1848, poet and man of letters, b. at Tyddyn Siôn, Abererch, Caerns.
98 This had been declaimed by M. Rio in his address to the society at the previous year's anniversary
99 *The Silurian*
100 Apollonia Rio (née Jones)

erable execution, particularly with her left hand'[101] but 'her natural timidity … prevented her doing … justice to her performance'. Susannah was the daughter of Mrs Prichard, who was *Carnhuanawc's* housekeeper, and it was he who taught Susannah to play.

Possibly Augusta Charlotte Elizabeth Hall, later Mrs Herbert

Image reproduced by kind permission of
Cambridge Harp Association

That night a ball was held at the Angel Inn, Abergavenny. Welsh was spoken by 'several ladies and gentlemen, of the first families in the Principality.' Beautiful coloured engravings[102] of the costumes of Wales were hung around the room and there was dancing and singing, and the 'fine old beverage of our ancestors', *Metheglin,*[103] was handed round.

When the company had left the room, it was reported that an *englyn,* written in English, had been found, discarded and lying on the floor.

*To those who know not what a **Welsh** Englyn is, this may give them a faint idea of its peculiar metre and style –*

The gout is about me most bitter, –
tearing
My toes like a tiger,
Its ire and its anger,
And keen bite, who can bear?
TWM JONES *a'i cant*

The alliteration even in this, is pretty, but some of the Welsh Englynion are transcendently beautiful.[104]

Some years earlier the following had appeared in *The Times.*

At the Royal Eisteddfod…held in Powys on Thursday…the Rev. Walter Davies, of Manafon, delivered the following report upon the poetical

---

101   The triple harp was played on the left shoulder, the left hand playing the higher strings
102   Probably the prints mentioned in a letter from Thomas Price to Taliesin Williams dated 12th August 1834.
     NLWJ Vol. XXXIV No. 2, 2007 'Lady Llanover and the Welsh Costume Prints', Michael Freeman
103   *Metheglin,* an alcoholic liquor made of fermented honey
104   *The Silurian*

compositions, which will, no doubt, prove highly edifying to those who can comprehend it:–

'The distinguishing character of Cambrian poetry … is that of a complicated rhyme called Cynghaned [sic] or alliterative-symphony of consonants rendered harmonious by a correspondent antiphony of vowel sounds. Whether this be the most eligible mode of composing Welsh verse is the point at issue between our modern sectaries. We must, however, beg leave to state, that when a happy idea is conveyed by cynghaned [sic] through the auricular portal to the judgement-hall of the sensorium, where is seated the angelic mind, with a swiftness outstripping the swift-winged arrows of light, the effect of such a concomitant and instantaneous influence upon Cambrian taste is scarcely describable!!!'

At this meeting of the Abergavenny Cymreigyddion Mr Williams of Aberpergwm suggested the formation of a society to promote Welsh literature by printing previously unpublished manuscripts. He was supported by Sir Charles Morgan, the Marquis of Bute and the Bishop of Llandaff, and it was expected that 'every nobleman and gentleman in Wales' would help to attain their objective. So the Welsh Manuscripts Society was established.

The remarkable Manuel boys were present at the Eisteddfod, and in the evening went to Llanover where everyone was very impressed by their intelligence and good manners. Mrs Waddington and the Halls decided to help the family by giving Mr Manuel a job as a gardener and a cottage for his family to live in and arranging for Mrs Manuel to give Welsh lessons to young Augusta Charlotte Elizabeth.[105]

Very soon after this Eisteddfod a tremendous storm caused serious damage at Llanover and the new house, nearing completion, did not escape its effects.

From all parts we have intelligence of the dreadful effects of the storm in the beginning of the week. The damage done is immense and greater than has ever been caused by any gale within the memory of man. The tremendous storm of Tuesday blew in the whole of the drawing room window of Llanover; and in half an hour thirty of the finest trees on the estate were prostrate, besides nearly half the apple trees in an old orchard. Damage was also done to the windows of the new house, and part of the lead torn from the roof.[106]

Benjamin had fought three general elections as candidate for the

---

105 *Presenting Monmouthshire No. 14, Autumn 1962* 'Child Prodigies at Llanover' Maxwell Fraser
106 *The Silurian*

Monmouthshire Boroughs. These had involved him in a great deal of expense so at the general election in June 1837, encouraged by the Liberal Committee of St Marylebone, he accepted their invitation to stand as candidate for that borough. He was duly elected, and performed his duties so well over the years that apart from one occasion, he was unopposed in later elections. The electors of Marylebone showed their appreciation in 1852 by meeting his costs during the election that year.

Despite the storm damage of the previous year *Llys Llanofer* was completed in time for the house-warming party, which was also a party welcoming the visitors to the Abergavenny Cymreigyddion Eisteddfod. This was held in the Free Grammar School-room on Wednesday the 18th and Thursday the 19th October 1837 with Benjamin Hall as President and *Carnhuanawc* as sole judge of the 'literary prose essays.'

A short while before the Eisteddfod the Rev. Walter Davies wrote to *Carnhuanawc* regarding Welsh music. A 'Teutonic' gentleman, who had become 'deeply enamoured with the scenery … and music of Wales' had drawn his attention to the way in which Welsh music was becoming distorted by 'Italianized taste'. The gentleman thought that something should be done to preserve Welsh music's original simplicity, and with this in mind the Rev. Davies suggested a scheme be submitted to the Abergavenny Cymreigyddion.

> *… that an establishment should be founded for the purpose of instructing a certain number of students, natives of South and North Wales, possessing musical genius, to play upon the Welsh harp in its own peculiar style.*
>
> *Sound the meeting, especially the musical part of it, from Titley Court to Llanover, Dowlais, Aberpergwm, &c.; and it is hoped that they will see the propriety of preserving, unmutilated, our native Welsh music in all the departments of the Principality.* [107]

John Jones, the harper, had sent 'the music' to the secretary but was perturbed at not hearing from Mr Bevan by the 9th October. He was anxious to know the dates of the Eisteddfod in order to make the necessary arrangements and begged 'the favour of an answer by return of Post.' [108]

One of the competitions judged on the first day of the meeting was for 'the best collection of unpublished Welsh music'. Miss Jane Williams [109] of

---

107   *The Literary Remains of the Rev. Thomas Price, Carnhuanawc*, ed. Jane Williams *(Ysgafell)*

108   NLW Ref. 13182-3E, letter dated 9th October 1837

109   Maria Jane Williams, *Llinos*, not to be confused with Jane Williams, *Ysgafell*, of Talgarth

Aberpergwm, was considered the better of the two entrants and was awarded the prize. Another competition was for 'the best specimen of real Welsh flannel, or woollen, in colours, and woven in any of the national check or stripes.' There were ten entries for this and the entry by Mrs Ann Harris[110] of Llanover was considered the best.

The young Victoria ascended the throne in June 1837 on the death of her uncle William IV,[111] and her coronation took place on 28th June 1838. In the Coronation Honours List Benjamin Hall's achievements were acknowledged and he was created a baronet.[112] How happy Augusta must have been to see her dear Benjamin so acknowledged; and, no doubt, not a little pleased at her own rise in status!

---

110   Ann Harris, 1786–?, Glyn Gwenffrwd, Llanover (Lower). From the 1841 census

111   William IV, 1765–1837, 3rd son of George III

112   *Hampshire Telegraph and Sussex Chronicle*

Chapter 3

Sir Benjamin and Lady Hall
(1838-1859)

*Gwenynen Gwent, or 'The Bee of Gwent'. The title is apt enough; for Lady Hall ...
is proverbially one of the busiest of her sex in all that relates to the welfare of her
poorer neighbours.*[1]

*The Anglicised Cymry, a class she detested ... smiled loftily at her efforts to preserve
the old wine of Wales, and would have it the 'bee' alluded to in her nom-de-plume
was 'in her bonnet'.*[2]

Mr Williams[3] of Aberpergwm had arranged for a little blind girl to have
harp tuition from John Jones who, at that time, was living in Clifton,
Bristol. It was Mr Williams's intention that the child should play at the meeting of the Cymreigyddion Society, which was to take place on the 10th and
11th October 1838. As John Jones was going to be there it was expected that
he would bring the little girl with him.

Mr Bevan, secretary of the Society, wrote to John Jones asking him to be in
Abergavenny well before the first day of the Eisteddfod. The harper was worried about the extra expense he would incur in having his pupil with him for
such a long time and replied to Mr Bevan saying that he would be in Abergavenny three or four days before the event and hoped that that would suf-
fice. Also he had arranged to meet Bassett Jones, the Cardiff harp maker, at
Newport, and travel with him to Abergavenny. However, he was willing to
change his arrangements and be there on the Thursday before the Eisteddfod.[4]

Sir Charles Morgan, Tredegar, presided at this meeting and *Carnhuanawc*
reported with pleasure that Armorica [Brittany] had sent a deputation to the
meeting. The King of France, King Louis Phillippe, had approved the visit to
Abergavenny by the Comte de Villemarqué[5] and four other Breton noblemen.
M. Rio and his wife were also present.

---

1   *The Atlantic Magazine,* 'A Welsh Musical Festival'.
2   Owen Morgan, Morien, 1836?–1921, Western Mail
3   Probably William Williams, 1788–1855, of Aberpergwm, Vale of Neath
4   NLW Ref. 13182-3E, letters dated 26th September and 2nd October 1838
5   Théodore Hersart de Villemarqué, 1815–1895

At the dinner on the second day Sir Charles Morgan presented the Comte with a Hirlas Horn,[6] and, accepting the gift on behalf of his fellow Bretons, the Comte replied …

… in my old age I will show this to my children and will tell them, 'It is the gift of our Welsh Brothers – learn like them to love your God, your country, your language and liberty.'

Ein Duw, ein Bro, ein Braint, ein Iaith[7]
[Our God, our Country, our Privilege, our Language]

Described as 'Pan Celtic', this meeting is regarded as the first modern Celtic Congress.[8]

Lady Greenly, that ardent supporter of everything Welsh, was not well enough to attend and, sadly, she died at the beginning of the following year.

A few months later, in June 1839, Sir Benjamin's mother, Mrs Hawkins, died but this does not seem to have affected the family very greatly. Sir Benjamin's references to Mr Hawkins in a journal (1822) suggest that he was not on good terms with him, and although Mrs Hawkins visited the Halls frequently her husband was never with her.

In St Nicholas Church in Brighton there is a tablet to Mrs Hawkins' memory, which reads:

Sacred to the memory of Charlotte
The beloved wife of Samuel Hawkins, Esq., of Shidfield, Wickham, Hants.,
Daughter of Richard Crawshay, Esq., of Merthyr, Glamorgan
and widow of Benjamin Hall, Esq., M.P., of Hensol Castle in the same county.
She died at Brighton June 8th, 1839, aged 55 years.

That year the anniversary of the Society was not publicly celebrated; Jane Williams, in the *Literary Remains of the Rev. Thomas Price*, remarked:

… the more immediate objects of Cymreigyddion institutions had, previous to the year 1840, been gradually lost sight of by the Abergavenny Committee. Subjects were no longer proposed and periodically discussed at the monthly meetings; and the local Eisteddfodau, which at first arose out of the literary association of the native townspeople, had already in effect, though undesignedly, supplanted it.

---

6 Horn of Plenty
7 *The Literary Remains of the Rev. Thomas Price, Carnhuanawc*, ed. Jane Williams (Ysgafell)
8 *Celtic Dawn*, Peter Berresford Ellis

In 1840, the seventh anniversary 'shone forth with accumulated strength and lustre'[9] with Mr John Rolls of the Hendre presiding. It was a grand affair, held on the 7th and 8th October, and a crowd of over 7000 formed the procession that greeted the president.[10]

Professor Albert Schulz[11] won a prize of eighty guineas for his essay on *The Influence of Welsh Traditions on the Literature of Germany, France and Scandinavia* the entries having been judged by Carl Bunsen who, in a letter to Lady Hall, wrote:

MY DEAR GWENYNEN GWENT,– You are a most lucky person, for you and your Cymreigyddion have obtained two treatises, of a quality such as any of the first Academies would esteem themselves fortunate in obtaining singly.[12]

Bunsen had received three essays, the first of which he dismissed as 'a superficial and dull essay', but of the other two he found it almost impossible to place one above the other, such was their merit. Eventually he decided in favour of the work of Professor Schulz.

The newly appointed Bishop of St David's, Connop Thirlwall,[13] was invited by Sir Benjamin to stay at Llanover and to attend the Eisteddfod. He was the first bishop of a Welsh Diocese to support the Abergavenny Cymreigyddion and had begun to learn Welsh very soon after his appointment.

It is stated that the Abergavenny Cymreigyddion is to be honoured by the presence of the learned Bishop of St. David's: it is also understood that his lordship is applying himself with zeal and ardour to the study of the Welsh language.[14]

The Bishop himself wrote:

I am learning Welsh faster than I expected … I am going next month to the Cymriggigian [sic] … I am to be Sir B. Hall's guest.[15]

His speech at the meeting, which was given in English, greatly impressed the assembly. The sentiments he expressed were similar to those of the Chevalier Bunsen at the 1838 Eisteddfod, who said, 'It is all very delightful and very beautiful, but … we must not let it end with the amusement of the day.' The Bishop's remarks were, '… this was only the steam to put the machine in

9   *The Literary Remains of the Rev. Thomas Price, Carnhuanawc,* ed. Jane Williams (Ysgafell)

10   *NLWJ Vol. XIV No. 1 Summer 1965,* 'Sir Benjamin and Lady Hall in the 1840s', Maxwell Fraser

11   Albert Schulz, San–Marté, 1802–1893

12   *A Memoir of Baron Bunsen,* letter dated 27th September 1840

13   Connop Thirlwall, 1797–1875

14   *The Bristol Mercury*

15   *NLWJ Vol. XIV No. 1 Summer 1965* 'Sir Benjamin and Lady Hall in the 1840s', Maxwell Fraser

motion, and to propel the engine', and *Carnhuanawc* ended the proceedings thus:

> *Now, Mr. President, Ladies, and Gentlemen, we trust that we have put on that steam, and also hitched on a train, laden with consequences of the most important character.*[16]

His words did not go unheeded and the monthly meetings of the Society began again with renewed vigour.

Sir Benjamin Hall was a fine-looking, well-dressed man and although he was no 'dandy' he was concerned with quality. When David Williams,[17] the woollen manufacturer who made the flannel for Sir Benjamin's trousers, decided to emigrate to New South Wales, Australia, Sir Benjamin was concerned that he would not be able to acquire such good material. In October 1841 David Williams, *Morgrygun*, [sic – possibly *Morgrugyn* – ant] wrote to his brother from Bristol, just before departing for Cork on his way to Australia with his wife and child.

> *I wish you to tell Mr. J. Harries to make, as quickly as possible, a specimen of the flannel used for Sir Benjamin Hall's trousers. The morning I left Llanover Sir Benjamin sent me a message to ask if my worker could make the material as good as I could as he was worried that Harries could not make the first one as good. – He wants a lot of it –*[18]

At this time there were at least two other woollen manufacturers in Llanover.

1841 Census for Llanover (Lower)

1. Tŷ To Maen:

William ROBERTS	age 50	Woolen [sic] Manufacturer	not born in county
Mary ROBERTS	age 40		not born in county
Daniel ROBERTS	age 15		not born in county
William ROBERTS	age 10		not born in county
Mary ROBERTS	age 7		not born in county
John PRICE	age 15		not born in county
David PRICE	age 15	Weaver	not born in county
Edward PRICE	age 14	Weaver	not born in county
Thomas EDWARDS	age 50	Carder	not born in county
Thomas JAMES	age 25	Weaver	not born in county

---

16 *The Literary Remains of the Rev. Thomas Price, Carnhuanawc,* ed. Jane Williams (Ysgafell)
17 David Williams, 1804?–1889, born in Carmarthenshire
18 Letter dated October 12th 1841. I am grateful to Ann Hall for permission to use this excerpt

2. Glyn Gwenffrwd:

Ann HARRIS	age 55	Woolen [sic] Manufacturer	born in county
James HARRIS	age 25	Weaver	born in county
Samuel HARRIS	age 25	Weaver	born in county
George HARRIS	age 20	Weaver	born in county
David ROBERTS	age 55	Weaver	born in county
Jeremiah MANSEL	age 50	Weaver	born in county
Evan EVANS	age 25	Spiner [sic]	born in county
William MORGAN	age 15	Winder	born in county
Phillip JONES	age 15	Carder	born in county
Isaac REES	age 10	Joiner	born in county
Ann JACOBS	age 15	Female Servant	born in county
Mary LEWIS	age 15	Female Servant	born in county
Hannah ROSSER	age 10	Female Servant	born in county
Jane SERVINI	age 10	Female Servant	born in county
Catherine MATHEWS	age 40	Washerwoman	born in county

Sir Benjamin was very active in Parliament during 1842, firmly stating his views on those subjects of most interest to him.

He has always professed ultra-liberal opinions, (supporting the ballot, and extension of the suffrage, and opposing centralization and the union of Church and State) [19]

In July he was one of a number of 'noblemen and gentlemen connected with the Principality' [20] who attended a meeting at the Thatched House Tavern, St James's, London. There they heard the report of a committee, appointed the previous year, regarding the establishment of a church where services would be held in the Welsh language. The Earl of Powis was the chairman and others attending the meeting included the Bishop of Bangor, Lord Dynevor and Sir W. W. Wynn. At first it had been proposed to build a church, but as only £2,250 had been raised it was thought better to rent somewhere. With this in mind negotiations had begun with the owners of the Episcopal Chapel, Ely Place, Holborn. In order that a clergyman's stipend could be secured a subscription was opened. Over a quarter of the required amount was raised there and then, with Sir Benjamin and several others each guaranteeing the sum of £10 annually.

Sir Benjamin went to Scotland in August to indulge in one of the sporting pastimes at which he excelled – shooting.

---

19   *The New York Times*
20   *The North Wales Chronicle*

It was when stalking deer, on one of his many visits to Scotland, that Sir Benjamin had the extraordinary experience of hitting two stags with one bullet, which pierced the throat of one, and killed another standing behind it.[21]

In the autumn Lady Hall was busy with preparations for the 9th anniversary of the Cymreigyddion Society. The Hindoo Prince Dwarkanauth Tagore[22] had been invited to the Eisteddfod but was unable to attend. Instead he sent his nephew, who accepted an illuminated address on his uncle's behalf. At this meeting, held on 12th and 13th October under the Presidency of Rhys Powell,[23] a prize of £5, offered by Lady Hall for the 'best Englynion[24] in honour of Dwarkanauth Tagore' was awarded to the Rev. James James, *Iago Emlyn,* who had already been awarded the prize for the best Englynion in honour of the Prince of Wales. The late Lady Greenly was not forgotten and a prize of £30 was awarded for the best poetical composition to her memory; the Rev. John Jones, *Tegid,* won the prize. There was also a prize of 5 guineas for the best Welsh ode on the visit of the Armorican [Breton] gentlemen to the Eisteddfod in 1838; and the great prize of 60 guineas was awarded to Carl Meyer for his essay on 'the place which the Welsh language occupies among the languages of the Indo-European race.' Prizes were also awarded for articles of woollen manufacture, with only real Welsh woollens and Welsh patterns being allowed.

The harp competition caused great interest, with nine harpers competing for four triple harps. The first prize, a new triple harp, value twenty guineas, was awarded to Miss Woodall of Monmouth, the second, value ten guineas, to John Fisher of Tredegar, the third, value ten guineas to Miss Nicholas of Abergavenny, and the last, value eight guineas, to Mr Jones 'late of Clifton'. Could this be John Jones, the harper who won the prestigious silver harp at the Brecon Eisteddfod of 1826 and was probably by this time the Llanover family harper?

The sumptuous dinner provided at the Angel Inn concluded with the 'national dish of toasted cheese washed down with a bowl of spiced ale.'[25]

Carnhuanawc's report on the progress of the Welsh Manuscripts Society aroused great interest. Its first publication was the *Liber Landavensis* [the Book

---

21 *NLWJ Vol. XIV No. 1 Summer 1965* 'Sir Benjamin and Lady Hall in the 1840s', Maxwell Fraser

22 Dwarkanauth Tagore, 1795–1846. He is buried in Kensal Green Cemetery

23 Rhys Davies Powell, 1801–1862, who built Craig-y-Nos Castle in 1842

24 Englynion (plural of englyn – Welsh alliterative stanza of four lines written in strict metre)

25 *The Bristol Mercury*

of Llandaff], which, he said, was 'not only valuable as an antiquarian document, but evidence that the banks of the Towy are not less fertile in the works of art than those of the Thames or Seine.'[26] The editor, Mr Rees, vicar of Casgob, Radnorshire, was busy preparing two more publications for the press; Sir Benjamin's sister Mrs Berrington's English translation of Schulz's prize winning essay of the previous Eisteddfod had already been published by Mr Rees of Tonn;[27] and work on preparing the manuscripts of *Iolo Morganwg*[28] for the press was making progress. Then *Carnhuanawc* paid tribute to Lady Charlotte Guest[29] for her work in translating the *Mabinogion* saying:

> ... *although the Society cannot prefer any direct claim, yet from its past undertaking having been suggested by the proceedings of one of our Eisteddfodau, the Cymreigyddion feel a pride in associating The Mabinogion, with their publications.*[30]

When Lady Charlotte Guest came to live in Dowlais, Glamorganshire, following her marriage to Josiah John Guest, the ironmaster, she showed an enthusiasm for all things Welsh. This naturally gained the approval of Lady Hall and her circle and she was always warmly welcomed at Llanover. She was introduced to the Rev. John Jones, *Tegid,* by Lady Hall and soon he began to instruct her in the Welsh language. The Llanover circle followed her progress with interest and when she declared her intention of translating the stories of the Mabinogion into English they gave her their whole-hearted support. The first volume was published in 1838, and the task took her eight years to complete, during which time she bore several children and also helped her husband in his business.

In spite of the warmth of her acceptance into the Llanover circle and the help and support they freely gave her, she made no acknowledgement in either her introduction to the work, or in her notes.

> It is only in her diaries ... that there is some indication of how deeply she was indebted to Tegid, Carnhuanawc, and to Mr Justice Bosanquet (another frequent visitor to Llanover.)[31]

---

26 *NLWJ Vol. XIV No. 1 Summer 1965* 'Sir Benjamin and Lady Hall in the 1840s', Maxwell Fraser

27 William Rees, 1808–1873, printer and publisher, Tonn, near Llandovery

28 Edward Williams, *Iolo Morganwg,* 1747–1826

29 Lady Charlotte Guest, née Bertie, 1812–1895, married in 1833 Josiah John Guest, 1785-1852; he was created a baronet in the Coronation Honours List, 1838

30 NLWJ Vol. XIV No. 1 Summer 1965 'Sir Benjamin and Lady Hall in the 1840s', Maxwell Fraser

31 *[T]ransactions of the [H]onourable [S]ociety of [C]ymmrodorion, Session 1968,* 'Lady Llanover and Her Circle' Maxwell Fraser

Lady Charlotte later complained that Lady Hall had shown her 'personal coolness amounting almost to incivility'. According to Maxwell Fraser Lady Charlotte was a remarkable businesswoman and shrewd in her judgements 'but there is no doubt that she was extremely neurotic.' In various entries in her diary she contradicted herself and 'it would be possible to quote many instances … showing her ability to dramatize herself to a ridiculous extent.' Although admitting she could not correctly recall a conversation with Lady Hall's mother, Mrs Waddington, she wrote about Mrs Waddington complaining of being neglected by her former friends at Court after marrying Mr Waddington, a man whose wealth had come from trade; but Mrs Waddington had been very kindly received by these friends. Maybe, since Lady Charlotte herself was very conscious of having 'married beneath her', she was only too ready to imagine a slight and to transfer these impressions to a third party.

Something that would have hurt Lady Hall deeply was a diary entry implying that Sir Benjamin had been unfaithful, and that she had been very grateful for Lady Charlotte's sympathy at that time. Apart from it being very unlikely that Lady Hall would have discussed anything so personal, or that she would have sought sympathy from anyone, everything points to the Halls' marriage being very secure and happy.

Maybe Lady Hall's 'coolness', if that is what it was, was due to the fact that following her marriage to Charles Schreiber, her children's tutor, Lady Charlotte abandoned every interest in Wales. She admits as much in her diary in an entry made in 1857.

He [Tennyson] talked a great deal about Welsh literature, and I, who have forgotten all the little I ever knew about that and everything else, felt quite ashamed at my own ignorance.[32]

At least she had the grace to feel ashamed!

When the Prince of Wales was just 2 years old Queen Victoria commanded *Carnhuanawc* to have a triple harp made for him, and to take it to London with two Welsh harpers. Bassett Jones of Cardiff, the favoured harp maker of the Abergavenny Cymreigyddion Society, made the harp and John Jones, by now established as the domestic harper at Llanover, and his pupil Thomas Gruffydd of Tredegar, accompanied *Carnhuanawc* to make the presentation. On July 27th 1843 the three Welshmen appeared before the Royal family and their eminent guests at Buckingham Palace. The harp was a magnificent

---

32   ibid

instrument, measuring about 6 feet high and 'elaborately carved in solid wood'. At the base of the pillar was 'the leek, intermingled with mistletoe and oak leaves' and at the top the Prince of Wales's feathers .[33]

Mr Price explained the intricacies of the ancient instrument to her Majesty and Prince Albert, both of whom showed an interest in the 'national minstrelsie of Wales'. Her Majesty was 'no stranger to the tones of the Welsh harp'[34] having heard it when she visited the Beaumaris Eisteddfod in 1832. John Jones played the *March of the Men of Harlech* 'in a masterly manner as well as with delicate taste and effect' on the Prince of Wales's harp, he and *Gruffydd* played duets on their own harps, and the performance ended with *Gruffydd* playing his own composition *Difyrwch Tywysog Cymru* [the Prince of Wales's Delight]. The Queen was so pleased with the whole affair that the harpers were each given twenty pounds and Bassett Jones became 'Welsh harpmaker to her Majesty and his Royal Highness Prince Albert'.

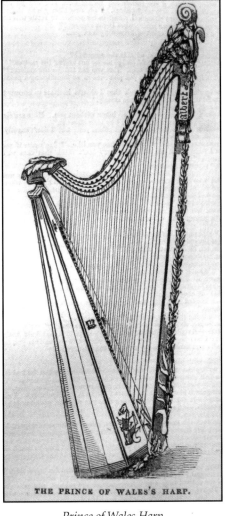

THE PRINCE OF WALES'S HARP.

Prince of Wales Harp

Illustrated London News: Photograph John Weedy

Just before Christmas 1843 the Church in Ely Place held its first services in Welsh. There is no mention of the Halls in the newspaper report but there is little doubt that they would have been very pleased at this. According to *The North Wales Chronicle* 'no event of late years created such a sensation among the Welsh residents in London.' The Church was crowded for both morning and evening services and the congregation listened intently to the service, which was read clearly and effectively by Mr Williams, the appointed minister.

---

33 *The Literary Remains of the Rev. Thomas Price, Carnhuanawc*, ed. Jane Williams (Ysgafell)

34 *Illustrated London News*

At the end of May the following year the congregation at the Church 'seemed electrified' when the Bishop of St David's preached a sermon there in Welsh, 'it being probably the first time that a Bishop had ever preached in Welsh in London, and that Bishop, too, an Englishman.'[35]

The collection of Welsh airs by Jane Williams, *Llinos*, which won the prize at the 1837 Abergavenny Eisteddfod, was published in 1844 under the title *Ancient National Airs of Gwent and Morganwg*. She had been planning this for some time and Lady Hall had received permission from the Queen for the volume to be dedicated to Her Majesty. She had promised that it would be a collection of Welsh airs with Welsh words, and although efforts were made to persuade Lady Hall that the books would not sell, as the Welsh words could not be translated adequately, she stood her ground. She enlisted the aid of *Taliesin ab Iolo*,[36] without Jane's knowledge, and finally her Ladyship had her way!

Lady Hall's brother-in-law, Carl Bunsen, had been appointed Prussian Minister at the Court of St James in 1841. When the Prince of Prussia[37] came to England in 1844, Carl Bunsen asked his sister-in-law, Lady Hall, to act as hostess at the dinner and ball given in the Prince's honour as his wife, Lady Hall's sister Frances, was staying on the Continent at the time. *The Morning Chronicle* of August 17th carried a very full report of the 'Fete to His Royal Highness the Prince of Prussia at the Chevalier Bunsen's residence.' The banquet was served in the dining room, where the table was decorated with flowers and fruit in gold receptacles, and large silver candelabra were arranged along the middle of the table. While the guests ate, a band played in the adjoining library. Over thirty people sat at the table, among them the Duke and Duchess of Cambridge and the Duke of Wellington. Lady Hall sat on the left of the Duke of Cambridge, and the Marchioness of Londonderry on his right.

After the meal came the usual toasts; the Prince of Prussia proposed the health of the Queen and the band played the National Anthem; Chevalier Bunsen toasted 'the Queen Dowager and the rest of the Royal Family' after which *Rule Britannia* was played. Finally the Prince rose to his feet once more and, offering his hand to the Duke of Wellington, gave the toast, 'The Health of the Duke of Wellington, the hero of Waterloo', whereupon the band struck up the appropriate tune *See the Conquering Hero Comes*.

---

35 *The Derby Mercury*
36 Taliesin Williams, Taliesin ab Iolo, 1787–1847, son of Iolo Morganwg
37 Prince William of Prussia, 1798–1888

The toasts over, it was time for the ladies to retire 'to take tea and coffee previous to the ball.' Three rooms were thrown open for the event with the dancing taking place in the suitably decorated saloon and the guests began to arrive at ten o'clock, foreign ambassadors and ministers among them. Some of the older guests left early but …

> '… the festivities of the night were prolonged some hours beyond midnight, the spirited strains of Collinet's band rendering the pleasures of the dance of the highest possible attraction.'

When his visit to London came to an end the Prince called on Lady Hall and her daughter to take his leave.[38] He was impressed with Lady Hall's charm and he never forgot how kind she was to him during his visit.[39]

On 1st September 1844 the *Sportsman's Gazette* reported that they had a 'rather indifferent account of the sporting upon the Monmouthshire Hills … the biped poachers having made the birds exceedingly scarce', but this did not worry Sir Benjamin; while his wife was busy in London entertaining royalty he was in Scotland for the shooting! The reports from there were very favourable, with Sir Benjamin bagging 69 brace one day, and several others bagging over 40 brace. All it needed was for the weather to become more favourable for it to become 'one of the most memorable seasons in the annals of grouse shooting.' While in Scotland Sir Benjamin visited the Braemar Gathering, as he frequently did.

Sir Benjamin and Lady Hall's son Hanbury was never very strong and in that year he suffered from a very painful illness, and while the family were in London for the Season Lady Hall nursed the ailing young man with her usual loving care. By October he was showing no sign of improvement so it was decided to take him home in the hope that the good Llanover air would benefit him, but to no avail. On the 11th February 1845, at *Llys Llanofer*, Hanbury died, the cause of death being 'dropsy of the head' [encephalitis].

There had already been an air of sadness surrounding Llanover when, in December 1844, John Jones died from pulmonary tuberculosis. He was buried in the churchyard at St Bartholomew's, Llanover, where his grave can still be seen, his impeccable lineage as a Welsh harper engraved in Welsh on the headstone, together with an image of a harp radiating its sweet cadences to the surrounding countryside; a fine memorial to a fine harper.

---

38 *The Morning Chronicle*
39 *NLWJ Vol. XIV No. 1 Summer 1965* 'Sir Benjamin and Lady Hall in the 1840s', Maxwell Fraser

It translates as follows:

Here lies John Jones, domestic harper to Sir B. Hall, of Llanover, Bart., and formerly of Dolgellau, Merioneth, who died December 12th,1844, aged 44. He excelled on the triple harp, and gained the silver harp at the Brecon Eisteddfod of 1826; and performed on the harp with applause before Her Majesty Queen Victoria, at the royal palace in 1843. He was a pupil of Richard Roberts, of Caernarvon; whose tutor was William Williams, of Penmorfa; whose tutor was John Parry, of Rhuabon, the original of Gray's Bard; whose tutor was Robert Parry, of Llanllyfni, in Arfon, who derived his art from the ancient harpers of Wales.

John Jones's Grave

*Faithful, courteous, gentle he went
Through the worldly course compelling;
And moved from here verily
To the choir of harpers above.*

*This tombstone was erected
by his widow Ellen Jones*

There was more worry for Lady Hall in June 1845 when Sir Benjamin was thrown from his horse, landing on his head. As a result he was unable to attend meetings of the parliamentary committees on which he sat. In the case of one of these, the business had already begun, but could not proceed as there was no-one to take his place and so a quorum could not be formed.[40] However, he recovered in time to preside at the twelfth anniversary of the Abergavenny Cymreigyddion, which was celebrated on 15th and 16th October 1845. It had been intended for Charles Morgan of Ruperra to be president, but due to his wife's illness he asked Sir Benjamin to take his place. Among the distinguished guests invited to stay at Llanover were Dr Carl Meyer, Librarian and Secretary to Prince Albert, representatives of the Diplomatic Corps, John Jones of Llanarth and Mr and Mrs Kemys-Tynte of Cefn Mably. Also present were the Rev. John Jones, *Tegid*, Maria Jane Williams, *Llinos*, and *Angharad Llwyd*.[41] Adding a touch of eastern mystery was Dwarkanauth

---

40 ibid
41 Angharad Llwyd, antiquary, 1780–1866. Tyn-y-Rhyl, Flintshire

Tagore, the public spirited Hindoo Prince who was a great benefactor in Calcutta and who had received many Royal favours since arriving in England. His family, however, did not approve of his European visits; in 1843 it had been announced in the *Bashkur*, the leading Hindoo journal of Calcutta, that 'the family of the Tagores had … resolved to punish their kinsman … for visiting Europe, by expulsion from their society'.

> *Dwarkanauth Tagore has been excluded from his family caste, in consequence of his repeatedly eating with "unclean Europeans."*[42]

Such was the success of the Society that by this time a new Cymreigyddion Hall had been built 'upwards of 100 feet in length, and of proportionate width and height.'[43] In spite of it having been thought large enough, it was filled to capacity for the Eisteddfod, with many unable to get in.

Abergavenny was bustling from early morning with people on horseback and in carriages, gathering for the meeting. Cannon were fired, church bells rang, flags flew and bands played. The procession formed about a mile outside the town, on the Monmouth road and wended its way to the town. There was a carriage carrying a working loom which caused much interest, and a 'very handsome car … [carrying] a miniature printing press, which was worked by two lads dressed in Welsh woollen'[44] and as they moved along about 400 leaflets were distributed to the onlookers, straight off the press. Closely following the procession were forty carriages carrying the President and his friends, the whole cavalcade extending for almost half a mile.

Procession passing the Angel Hotel   *Inside the Cymreigyddion Hall*

Illustrated London News: Photographs John Weedy

---

42 *The Manchester Times and Gazette*
43 *The Bristol Mercury*
44 *Illustrated London News*

Inside, the Hall was lit by chandeliers and lamps 'whose light shed a rich lustre' on the busy scene. The whole place was decorated with evergreens, and a crown and harps made of dahlias; other decorations included the Prince of Wales feathers and banners with the word *Cymry* in old Bardic figures. On one side of the platform stood a splendid marble statue of *Taliesin pen Beirdd*,[45] the work of Mr W. Jones of Merthyr Tydfil, which had been brought 150 miles to be displayed at the Eisteddfod. At mid-day the sound of a trumpet opened the Eisteddfod and the President took his seat to the music of a harp chorus.[46] There was such a rush of people anxious to get into the Hall that it was some time before the President could officially open the meeting, which eventually began with a small choir of six men and two women singing *Y Bardd yn ei Awen*. When they had finished *Carnhuanawc* got to his feet to huge applause. As on other occasions he drew attention to the literary works already published, such as Professor Schulz's great essay on *The Influence of Welsh Tradition on the Literature of Europe; Philological Proofs of the Unity of the Human Race* by A. H. Johnes; Lady Charlotte Guest's translation of the *Mabinogion*; the *Liber Landavensis*, and several others. He challenged any similar Society in the world to produce such an abundance of academic works and reminded his audience that the Society also patronised the loom, music, and the arts as demonstrated by the 'fine specimen of sculpture … shown at this Eisteddfod.' It must have been a pleasure for everyone to learn that their beloved *Carnhuanawc* had been awarded the great prize for his essay 'on the comparative merits of the remains of ancient literature in the Welsh, Irish, and Gaelic languages …'[47]

At the end of the day a vote of thanks was called for, to someone 'whose name was typified by "The Bee", and to whom they were deeply indebted for the pleasures of that day.'

Scarcely had the words escaped from his lips, when the Hall rung with most tremendous enthusiasm and reiterated cheering. Never was a compliment more richly merited, never one, nor ever will be another, more nobly responded to. The waving of hats and handkerchiefs, the uplifting of hearts and voices told truly in what profound respect and devotion the noble lady was held.[48]

Lady Hall's response was, 'My friends, my heart is in Wales and in Abergavenny; I thank you for the honour you have done me.'

---

45 *Taliesin pen Beirdd* (Chief Bard of Britain) lived in Wales during the last half of the sixth century
46 *Illustrated London News*
47 *NLWJ Vol. XIV No. 1 Summer 1965* 'Sir Benjamin and Lady Hall in the 1840s', Maxwell Fraser
48 *Illustrated London News*

When the time came for an address to be presented to Prince Dwarkanauth Tagore, their 'illustrious visitor', there was a surprise in store. David Williams of Cwmdu, a young man about 18 years old, had spent some time in the Prince's homeland and was able to address him in his own language. The Prince's acknowledgement was simple and heartfelt and was received with 'thunders of applause.' He recalled the address received on his behalf by his nephew at the previous Eisteddfod and said that, together with the one today, they would show his descendants that his visit had been 'well repaid by the honours [he received] from this most ancient and learned Society ... '[49]

The Prince never returned to his native land; in March the following year he was taken ill on his return to London from a visit to Paris. He was sufficiently recovered by the beginning of May to contemplate a visit to Brighton. *The Era* of 3rd May carried the news, continuing as follows:

> *The example given by this enlightened and clever man has had so beneficial an effect on his countrymen, that several of them propose visiting England ... [We may consequently expect in our drawing-rooms quite a glut of Baboos.[50] –Ed. Era.]*

A newspaper report[51] at the beginning of August wrote of the Prince's friends being alarmed as he was suffering from a 'severe attack of indisposition.' Two days later the same newspaper reported his death, which was caused by 'an infection of the liver.'

Sir Benjamin and Lady Hall's only surviving child, their daughter Augusta Charlotte Elizabeth, fell in love with John Arthur Edward Jones, of the nearby Llanarth estate. This seemed to echo their own 'boy and girl romance', the difference being that the Llanarth family were of the Roman Catholic faith. Tolerant as the Halls were of other faiths, it must have brought sad memories to Lady Hall of the ill-fated marriage of her sister Emelia. How she must have prayed that history would not be repeated, and that the marriage of their cherished daughter would be long and happy.

The marriage took place on the 12th November 1846 at the private chapel at Llanarth, followed by a Protestant ceremony in the Parish Church, Llanover. For days before the event the houses at Llanover and Llanarth were full to bursting point with relatives and friends.

---

49 *NLWJ Vol. XIV No. 1 Summer 1965* 'Sir Benjamin and Lady Hall in the 1840s', Maxwell Fraser
50 Baboo – Hindoo Gentleman
51 *Freeman's Journal and Daily Commercial Advertiser*

Taliesin Williams died early in 1847. It was his wish that his father's manuscripts be kept together and disposed of to the British Museum and the money given to his widow. However the British Museum did not want the collection. Lady Hall approached the institution on behalf of his family, but to no avail. The authorities wrote to Lady Hall stating that 'the Committee had deliberated on the Iolo MSS. and they had decided to have nothing to do with them.'[52] The manuscripts remained with Taliesin's widow in Merthyr for some time but by 1853 the family was in need of money, and Sir Benjamin, worried that the collection might be disposed of unsatisfactorily, bought the manuscripts and placed them in the library at Llanover.

That year, 1847, there was another General Election and Sir Benjamin was once again returned for Marylebone. In the same year Llandovery College, Carmarthenshire, was founded, thanks to Lady Hall who had given the land on which it was built, and who had encouraged Thomas Phillips[53] in his wish to create a Welsh educational establishment. It was also the year that saw the publication of the infamous *Blue Books*.

A Royal Commission had been set up to report on the state of education in Wales, especially into 'the means afforded to the labouring classes of acquiring a knowledge of the English language.'[54] The three commissioners may have been very capable and well intentioned, but they had no knowledge of the Welsh language. When they questioned the children it was in English, which the children did not understand and so could not answer correctly, if at all. So the children were said to be illiterate. The morals of the Welsh were also said to be questionable, and this was attributed to the fact that they were mostly Dissenters. When the report was published, in three great blue-bound volumes, it caused great resentment in Wales and even today there is much bitterness about *Brad y Llyfrau Gleision* - the Treachery of the Blue Books. The Halls were naturally extremely annoyed at this attack on Wales and the Welsh people, and encouraged Jane Williams,[55] *Ysgafell,* to examine the report and counter the conclusions arrived at by the commissioners.

In 1848 John Jones, the Halls' son-in-law, was given permission to change his name from Jones to the old family name of Herbert.

---

52 *NLWJ Vol. XIV No. 2 Winter 1965* 'Sir Benjamin and Lady Hall in the 1840s', Maxwell Fraser

53 Thomas Phillips, 1760–1851

54 *NLWJ Vol. XIV No. 2 Winter 1965* 'Sir Benjamin and Lady Hall in the 1840s', Maxwell Fraser

55 Jane Williams, *Ysgafell,* 1806–1885. She was descended from Henry Williams of Ysgafell, near Newtown, Montgomeryshire.

John Jones, with his brothers and only surviving sister[56] were 'especially and alone authorized by royal licence and sign-manual, September 20 1848, to adopt the surname of his illustrious ancestors (HERBERT), being the representative of the elder branch of the Herbert family in direct male descent for more than 800 years.'

The name Herbert had been lost in his branch of the family when, under English law, the Welsh were required to adopt fixed surnames. John Jones wrote to the head of the Herbert family, the Earl of Pembroke, informing him of his intention and asking if the Earl had any objection.

The Earl replied that he had not, but that if many others followed his example, he might be compelled to apply for permission to change his family name to Jones.[57]

The story may be spurious but the Llanarth Joneses were descended from a third son whereas the Earls of Pembroke were descended from a fourth son, thus the Joneses were the senior branch of the Herbert family.

The Halls spent a very happy time in Aberystwyth in the autumn of 1848 but when in Scotland for the shooting season Benjamin had a serious accident while out riding. Due to the resulting injury he needed to go to London to consult the best doctors there. This was the time when preparations for the Abergavenny Eisteddfod were under way so Augusta had a real dilemma – should she go to London to care for her injured husband or should she remain at Llanover to greet the people invited for the Eisteddfod and help with the preparations. The success of the Eisteddfod was very important to both of them and the decision was made for Lady Hall to stay at home and leave Sir Benjamin in the capable hands of the London doctors.

ACCIDENT TO SIR BENJAMIN HALL.–The reason Sir Benjamin Hall, Bart., was unable to attend the great Bardic gathering at Llanover was that he had a fall from his horse when riding over his Grouse Moors, in Aberdeenshire, and he has since been confined to his house under medical care.[58]

The Queen had given permission for the event to be held under the patronage of the Prince of Wales, and the list of eminent people staying at Llanover included Lady Hall's sister Frances and her husband the Chevalier

---

56   Arthur James Herbert, 1820-1897, Edmund Philip Herbert, 1823-1894,
     and Mary Louisa Herbert, 1831-?, m. John Hillier Tozer
57   *NLWJ Vol. XIV No. 2 Winter 1965* 'Sir Benjamin and Lady Hall in the 1840s', Maxwell Fraser
58   *Freeman's Journal* and *Daily Commercial Advertiser*

Bunsen, the Turkish Ambassador, Sir John and Lady Charlotte Guest, Archdeacon John Williams, Henry Hallam, the historian, Lady Morgan of Tredegar and Miss Morgan, Mr Williams of Aberpergwm and the two Miss Williamses, and *Angharad Llwyd*. The President was Colonel Kemys-Tynte, of Cefn Mably, who brought a house party to the Eisteddfod. One of these people, not understanding how committed the Halls were to ensuring the success of the Eisteddfod, wrote …

> *Sir Benjamin is in London and expected to lose one of his eyes, but her Ladyship it seems is not nervous about him and entertains company at home.*[59]

Lady Hall was not one to let her worries show, and as there was little she could do for her husband while he was under the care of the best doctors, she devoted her energies to the Eisteddfod. As usual *Carnhuanawc* spent several weeks at Llanover prior to the Eisteddfod although his health was giving cause for concern. Some months previously he had suffered a seizure which left him unconscious for several hours. Mr Wakeman, his medical advisor, was of the opinion 'that should a similar seizure recur, Mr. Price would not survive it.'[60] He never fully recovered but the change of air and the company of good friends at Llanover did much to lift his spirits. His friends were concerned to see him looking so feeble and although he had been warned not to

The Death of Tewdrig
Image reproduced by kind permission
of Brecon Museum

over exert himself he was as determined as Lady Hall to do everything he could to ensure the success of the event.

The Eisteddfod was held in the Cymreigyddion Hall in Abergavenny on Wednesday and Thursday, 11th and 12th October 1848. Because Sir Benjamin could not be there *Carnhuanawc* took his place as one of the judges of the sculpture competition, the other judge being Mr Williams of Aberpergwm. The prize of £70.10s (£20 of which was given by the late Dwarkanauth Tagore at the previous Eisteddfod) for the best plaster model 'illustrative of Cambro-British history' was awarded to John Evan Thomas of Brecon. He designed the model, depicting

---

59 *NLWJ Vol. XIV No. 2 Winter 1965* 'Sir Benjamin and Lady Hall in the 1840s', Maxwell Fraser
60 *The Literary Remains of the Rev. Thomas Price, Carnhuanawc*, ed. Jane Williams (Ysgafell)

the death of the 5th Century King Tewdrig, and his brother William Meredyth Thomas modelled it. In 1856 it was cast in bronze at Elkington & Co., Birmingham and is now on display in Brecon Museum.

The Prince of Wales had offered a prize of 25 guineas 'for the best critical essay on the history of the language and literature of Wales ... ' which was awarded to Thomas Stephens, a self-educated man from Merthyr.

The essay was subsequently published under the title of 'The Literature of the Cymry,' at the charge of the good and generous Sir J. John Guest.[61]

The prize of five guineas for the best essay on *The Statutes of Rhuddlan*, by which Wales was annexed to England, was awarded to *Carnhuanawc*, which must have raised his spirits and brought him much satisfaction; it was noted that on the second day of the meeting he was a little better.

Carnhuanawc

Paper Cutting by Lady Llanofer
Literary Remains of the Rev Thomas Price

He returned to Cwmdu utterly exhausted. In spite of constant sickness, which made it difficult for him to take enough nourishment, he got up every day and often walked in his favourite places. On the 7th November, Lady Hall, having heard of his continued illness, sent the two Miss Williamses of Aberpergwm to bring him back to Llanover. He and his visitors sat and conversed for a while on many subjects, and when the subject of music arose, *Carnhuanawc* went to get his favourite triple harp to illustrate his remarks. He then wrote a note to Lady Hall explaining that he was too ill to travel then, but hoped to be well enough soon to visit as he was anxious to see Sir Benjamin who himself was seriously ill. Having seen his visitors into their carriage he returned to the *Persondy* [Vicarage]. His housekeeper, Mrs Prichard was not at home and had left her eldest daughter, Elinor, in charge. She encouraged *Carnhuanawc* to take some food and he tried to eat. Elinor left him and, as she usually did at his meal-times, sat and played her harp. When she next went into his room

61 ibid

she found him leaning over in his chair, his head drooping and his eyes closed; he could not speak. Although greatly alarmed, the sensible girl tried to make him comfortable then sent for help. Dr Henry Lucas arrived, followed closely by Mr Wakeman but there was nothing they could do.

Mr. Price without uttering a word, or giving any distinct sign of consciousness, softly breathed his last the same evening, at half past eight o'clock.[62]

Young Elinor Prichard registered the death of this remarkable man, the cause of his death being given as 'serous apoplexy'. [Stroke accompanied by feeble pulse and pale countenance.]

1849 was spent quietly due to Sir Benjamin's accident[63] and there was more sadness for the family when, in January 1850, Mrs Waddington died suddenly. Although she had frequent spells of poor health, she had seemed better during the summer of 1849, so her death came as a shock. The marriage of Marie Bunsen, daughter of Carl and Frances Bunsen, to Mr J. B. Harford, which should have taken place in January, was postponed until April. By then Sir Benjamin had recovered from his problems of the previous year, and he proposed the health of the bridesmaids. His speech was very humorous and was received 'most enthusiastically.'[64]

The Welsh magazine for women, *Y Gymraes* [The Welshwoman] was published in 1850 by Ieuan Gwynedd, with the support of Lady Hall, and in the first edition she wrote, 'Mothers of Wales, speak Welsh to your children … It is from you, and not from their fathers, that they will learn to love God in their own language.' In the same year Sylvan Evans' dictionary was published, again with the support of Lady Hall.

The 20th Anniversary of the Abergavenny Cymreigyddion Society was celebrated with an Eisteddfod to which a number of distinguished guests were invited, many of whom stayed at Llanover enjoying the hospitality of Sir Benjamin and Lady Hall. The Eisteddfod was held on the 12th and 13th October, 1853, and was the first one to be organised since 1848. The usual procession formed outside the town and made its way to the Cymreigyddion Hall in Abergavenny, where a chorus of harps greeted it. Once everyone was settled the meeting was opened with the sound of a trumpet.

Charles Morgan, MP had been appointed President, but had asked Sir Ben-

---

62   *The Literary Remains of the Rev. Thomas Price, Carnhuanawc*, ed. Jane Williams (Ysgafell)
63   *THSC, Session 1964, Part I*, 'Lord Llanover (Big Ben) in London', Maxwell Fraser
64   *The Times*

jamin to take his place, due to 'an infliction of Providence.' Sir Benjamin explained the situation to the meeting saying, 'although he is now in a distant clime his *heart* is with us.'[65] In his opening address Sir Benjamin compared that day with the occasion 20 years previously saying, 'I believe that the procession only consisted of Lady Hall, myself, and about twenty other persons!' He hoped and believed that each year the numbers would increase and the enthusiasm remain undiminished.

When the Rev. David James, Warden of Llandovery College, gave his address he recalled the occasion, 15 years earlier, when young John Thomas[66] of Bridgend, had won the harp prize. This young boy's career had flourished, due in part to Countess Ada Lovelace, daughter of Lord Byron, who had used her influence to gain for him a place at the Royal Academy of Music, where he had studied the harp for six years. He had been well received as a performer on the Continent, and was now Professor of Harp at the Royal Academy of Music. He was one of the people staying at Llanover, and was the judge of the music competitions at that Eisteddfod, which ended optimistically with a list of proposed subjects for the next eisteddfod having been drawn up and an announcement of the prizes already promised.

Mrs Lucy[67] of Charlecote, and her son and daughter, Spencer and Caroline (Carry) were among those invited to stay at Llanover for the Eisteddfod. They arrived later than expected after 'a long and wearisome journey' and dinner was over. Nothing had been put aside for them and their maid could only find a slice of cold meat and some bread, which was soon devoured by the three hungry people. Carry was very tired and went to bed but Mrs Lucy and Spencer went downstairs to be greeted warmly by Sir Benjamin and Lady Hall. They were then introduced to the other guests amongst whom were 'the Count Esterhazy, the Duke of Somerset and his lovely daughter Lady Ulrica Somerset, Lady Langdale and her daughter Miss Bickensteth [sic] (an heiress), Sir John and Lady Shelley and their daughter, an heiress also.'

When Mrs Lucy returned to her room she found a note that read, 'A fly ordered to take you to the Eisteddfod each day during the week and the charge one guinea a day.' In her memoirs Mrs Lucy wrote, 'I thought to myself, this is a queer place, and so it seemed was the general opinion, and some wag wrote on their entrance gate, "A park without deer, a house without beer;

---

65   *The Cambrian Journal, Vol. 1, 1854*
66   John Thomas, *Pencerdd Gwalia*, 1826–1913
67   Mary Elizabeth Lucy (née Williams), b. at Boddlewyddan [sic], Flintshire, 25th Nov. 1803

Sir Benjamin Hall lives here."'

The next day a servant brought the ladies the 'frights' as Mrs Lucy called the flannel dress and tall hat that Lady Hall asked all her lady guests to wear to the Eisteddfod. 'All the ladies were furious but were putting on the Welsh dress etc. which Lady Hall had sent to each of them … I never was more uncomfortable…' After that uncomfortable first day Mrs Lucy vowed never again to 'wear such horrible things to please any Lady Hall, nor did I, and all the other ladies agreed with me and we returned our linsteys and hats etc. to her Ladyship that same evening and made her very angry.' On one occasion a large group of the guests were together in the drawing room …

> … where Sir Harry Vane and Spencer were very merry and making us all laugh (her ladyship was not present), when the door opened and Sir Benjamin, looking extremely grave, and the Duke of Somerset as stiff as a poker, walked in and said, 'I beg you will not all laugh so loud as I do not like noise,' and before we could recover from our astonishment and make any reply, he vanished and His Grace along with him.[68]

John Thomas, the young harpist, was staying at Llanover at the time, as he was to be Judge of Music at the Eisteddfod. Mrs Lucy heard him practising in 'a house in the park' [Ty Uchaf] and was captivated by his playing. She asked Lady Hall why she did not have him play for her guests as 'his playing was simply glorious'. 'But', wrote Mrs Lucy, 'the provoking and tyrannical woman said, "No, you would spoil him, he must keep in his room and study."'

At a ball in Abergavenny 'to which we all went, and Mr Thomas too', all the young ladies were very disappointed that the modest and gentlemanly young man was not allowed to dance, as Lady Hall disapproved of his dancing. He spent most of the evening sitting with Mrs Lucy who found

John Thomas Pencerdd Gwalia

Image reproduced by kind permission of Bridgend Library

him charming and according to her the two became 'life-long friends'. She also records a rumpus concerning Mr Thomas and his dancing when Mrs

---

68 *Mistress of Charlecote*, Alice Lady Fairfax-Lucy; Victor Gollancz Ltd., London 1983

Herbert, Sir Benjamin and Lady Hall's daughter, held a ball at Llanarth. One of the young ladies asked the young harpist to dance but he, saying he did not wish to annoy her Ladyship, declined. At this one of the guests remonstrated with him, saying, 'Nonsense, Mr Thomas, you cannot refuse a lady when she asks you to be her partner.' So he stood up and they danced together.

Lady Hall, seeing them, flew at him like a tigress and insisted on his retiring. Then we all attacked her and defended Mr. Thomas, Mrs. Herbert too came to the rescue and remonstrated with her mother and there was quite a scene. [69]

It seems Lady Hall did not have her own way in this instance as Mr Thomas danced for the rest of the evening, with no shortage of partners!

Soon after their meeting at Llanover Mrs Lucy began harp lessons with John Thomas. She had begun learning to play the harp when she was sixteen years old but must have been badly taught; although he complimented her on her fine tone he needed to correct her hand as she held it badly 'with your thumb down instead of up.' He wanted her to 'unlearn' what she had been taught so that he could make her 'a really fine player.'

After the Eisteddfod Sir Benjamin arranged an outing, which did not please young Spencer Lucy as he, and others, had been looking forward to some shooting. Everyone was told where they were to go 'regardless of their own wishes' and Mrs Lucy had what she considered the dubious honour of sitting beside Sir Benjamin in a dog cart, an arrangement that she found 'far from agreeable.' 'Sir Benjamin and his lady were anything but a genial host and hostess,' wrote Mrs Lucy in her memoirs, but perhaps the Lucy family were less than considerate guests! They arrived late at Llanover; Mrs Lucy and Carry objected to wearing the Welsh dress to the Eisteddfod and were the ringleaders of a 'revolt' by the rest of the ladies; Spencer Lucy was unhappy at the lack of shooting, and in spite of Sir Benjamin and Lady Hall not allowing smoking he, as well as other male guests, smoked in his bedroom.

Mrs Lucy's memoirs, which include this rather spiteful picture of Sir Benjamin and Lady Hall, were written when she was nearing the end of her long and eventful life. She had grown stout with age and suffered from rheumatism in her hands. She suffered from recurring bouts of bronchitis that left her weak and kept her more or less confined to the 'dear snug little room' that became her haven. Her memoirs give the impression that she was prone

---

69 *Mistress of Charlecote,* Alice Lady Fairfax-Lucy; Victor Gollancz Ltd., London 1983

to exaggeration. Maybe this tendency, together with the fact that the scenes she was describing had happened thirty years previously, rendered her memory unreliable. Her 'most dearly loved Carry', said to be very like her mother, seems to have been a silly girl, prone to fainting at the most inappropriate moments. Her first Drawing Room was almost a disaster, due to her fainting in 'the crowd and crush of ladies fat and lean'.

One incident, not recorded in Mrs Lucy's memoirs but noted in a diary, gave Carry a reputation for being rather 'fast'. She was walking home alone one day when Colonel Shirley of Ettington met her and offered to accompany her to Charlecote. Their conversation, Carry later admitted, was 'lively'[70] but nothing to be ashamed of. However, a labourer in a nearby field said he had seen her lying on the ground with her petticoats around her waist! He had also seen her 'drawers', and he said she did not seem to be struggling. Carry's version was that Colonel Shirley had tried to 'salute' her and she had become hysterical, collapsing on the ground. The poor 'insulted' girl rushed home in floods of tears and in the legal enquiry that followed it was said that she had become unconscious and had no idea of what had really happened. The jurors, all county neighbours of the Lucys, decided that the labourer had lied in the hope of receiving payment to keep his mouth shut and Carry was packed off to Wales until the whole affair had quietened down. Little wonder the very 'proper' Sir Benjamin and Lady Hall showed their disapproval of this frivolous family!

By an Act of Parliament in 1853, Christ College, Brecon, was refounded. Since the 1840s the school had been in such a bad state of repair that it had almost closed. It was thanks to influential people like Sir Benjamin, who wrote to the Archbishop of Canterbury demanding the school be repaired and renewed, that eventually this happened.[71]

In spite of the apparent success of the Abergavenny Cymreigyddion, at the meeting that took place in January 1854 the Society was dissolved. Had the stalwarts lost heart? So many of the supporters had died; Lady Greenly in 1839, Sir Charles Morgan in 1846, *Carnhuanawc* in 1848 and John Jones, *Tegid*, in 1852. Lady Hall's much-loved mother, Mrs Waddington had died in 1850 and Sir John and Lady Charlotte Guest had moved to Canford Manor in 1846, where Sir John died in 1852.

In 1854 and 1855 *The Literary Remains of the Rev. Thomas Price* was published

---

70 'possibly flirtatious' according to the editor of Mrs Lucy's memoirs
71 St David's Day lecture at Brecon Library, 2004 by Mr Edward Parry

in two volumes. It had been the intention of the Ven. John Williams, Archdeacon of Cardigan, to edit *Carnhuanawc's* papers but his busy schedule prevented him from doing so. As the publisher, Mr Rees of Tonn, Llandovery, and *Carnhuanawc's* friends were anxious to proceed with the task they asked Jane Williams, *Ysgafell*, to undertake it.

> *A mingled mass of unsorted papers, comprising the miscellaneous accumulations of more than fifty years, and including the principal materials for the present work, were, consequently delivered untouched to the present possessor.*[72]

Several of the drawings in the volumes are the work of Lady Hall; others are the work of her daughter, Mrs Herbert of Llanarth, C. Berrington [possibly Charlotte, Sir Benjamin's sister], and C. E. Lucas [possibly Caroline Lucas, later Lady Gardner Wilkinson].

At the end of the Parliamentary Session, in August 1854, Sir Benjamin and his colleague, Lord Dudley Stuart, attended a meeting of the vestry of St Marylebone where they received a vote of thanks for their efforts on behalf of the borough. Sir Benjamin had just been appointed Minister of Health and he was at pains to stress that in no way did he solicit the appointment. In fact, he had asked for time to consult his colleagues as to his suitability for the position. It was as a result of *their* wishes that he had accepted. He ended his speech with the hope that he would continue to be their representative for many years to come.[73]

Sir Benjamin Hall, Member for Marylebone, 1854

Within two weeks of his taking office cholera broke out in London, and Sir Benjamin soon demonstrated his administrative abilities. Not one to re-

---

72 *The Literary Remains of the Rev. Thomas Price, Carnhuanawc*, ed. Jane Williams (Ysgafell)
73 *The Times*

main at his desk and receive reports from others, he went to the East End of London to direct personally the work to combat the disease. He was so appalled by the conditions he found there that he piloted a bill through Parliament which was 'the turning point in the sanitary history and evolution of London,' and which resulted in the creation of the Metropolitan Board of Works, the fore-runner of the London County Council.[74] The Bill received Royal Assent in August 1855 but by then Sir Benjamin had taken up a new position.

The decline of the Church in Wales worried Sir Benjamin. He believed it was due to English or mixed services being held in parish churches and to the frequent appointment of ministers who did not understand the language or the character of the Welsh people. As a result the parishioners were deserting the Church and flocking to the Dissenting chapels where they received their religious instruction from Welsh ministers speaking eloquently in their own language.

NEW CHURCH, BUILT BY SIR BENJAMIN HALL, AT ABERCARN, SOUTH WALES.

The Welsh Church, Abercarn

Illustrated London News: Photograph John Weedy

Determined as always to further the cause of maintaining the language, and with the welfare of his tenants in mind, Sir Benjamin drew up plans for a new church to be erected on his estate at Abercarn.[75] It was built of local stone, in a simple style; the stone corbels and window mullions were finely sculpted but 'devoid of all fantastic ornaments'.

Inside, the roof was well proportioned, with solid cross-beams made of oak, as were the pulpit and communion rail. Sir Benjamin demonstrated the Halls' loyalty to the Crown by having the Royal Arms painted on the front of the gallery, and their determination that it should be a Welsh church by having the Commandments, the Creed and the Lord's Prayer displayed in Welsh in 'black letters on large slates, framed in oak, with gilt moulding.' The building was

74   *THSC, Session 1964, Part I,* 'Lord Llanover (Big Ben) in London', Maxwell Fraser
75   *Illustrated London News*

lit by four lanterns, suspended by chains from the roof, and warmed by hot water pipes running under the floor. The Church was intended for the use of Welsh-speaking people and Sir Benjamin had given orders that 'his Church should not be nominally, but actually, appropriated to the use of his country-men.' Everything had been done to benefit the Welsh people; they could now be sure that regular services would be held in their own language, by a Welsh-speaking minister who would be selected and maintained by Sir Benjamin, and who would devote himself to his Welsh congregation.[76]

The first Divine services were held in this warm, inviting church on Thursday 16th November 1854. A good road had been made to the church, which was in a fairly remote spot in the mountains above the village of Abergwyddon. The Bishop of Llandaff and the Rural Dean had been invited, and also those of the 'upper classes' who understood Welsh and who were 'deeply interested in the revival of the Church in Wales.' Local people, about a thousand in number, dressed in 'national costume', gathered outside awaiting the arrival of Sir Benjamin and Lady Hall, before entering the building themselves. The Halls and their party arrived about eleven o'clock, followed by their servants and behind them came the Welsh Chancellor of the diocese, the Rev. Hugh Williams with twenty Welsh clergymen.

Welsh Peasant Woman
Illustrated London News: Photograph John Weedy

At the end of the morning service nearly two hundred children from the Welsh Sunday School lined the road, and their master, a dissenter, cordially greeted the Bishop, in Welsh, as he passed. The guests walked the mile from the new church to the Halls' house where they had an early dinner. Then another service was held, at three o'clock, followed by light refreshments at Sir Benjamin's, and back to the Church for the evening service. This ended about ten o'clock, and it was reported that about two thousand people attended the three services. Demonstrating yet again his tolerance of others, Sir Benjamin 'lent his private chapel for the use of the English residents, who have service performed in it every Monday for themselves by another clergyman.'[77]

76 ibid
77 ibid

The membership of the Church of Jesus Christ of Latter-day Saints had been increasing in South Wales at that time. One family who converted was the Powell[78] family. John Powell was a stonemason on the Llanover estate and he became very ill with 'a strange sickness which spread through the village.' His wife Elizabeth had just given birth to a baby girl, her seventh child, and had to nurse him as none of the neighbours dared go near the house. The news reached Lady Hall, who, with her maid, called at the Powell's home and told Elizabeth to go and rest – **she** would give John his medicine. Elizabeth protested, but Lady Hall would have none of it, saying:

Your neighbours are willing at heart but they are frightened. They dare not come. As for me I'm glad to help you. I am not frightened. I can rest and sleep during the day. Eliza, you are not in the condition to wait on John. Lie down and get well.

Lady Hall went to the cottage and nursed John night after night, allowing Elizabeth to rest and look after the newborn child.

One night, when John's condition had worsened, the Mormon Elders arrived. Lady Hall was pleased to meet them and thought that their presence would help the sick man. 'You have come a long way to help a sick friend,' she said. 'Your actions speak louder than your words. It is a good religion that directs you.' The Elders promised John that he would get better, and that he would go to Utah and work on the Temple. He never regained his full strength and when he returned to work Sir Benjamin advised him to delegate the work, and to go home each day before sunset. In 1856 John decided to take his family to Utah. When he gave his notice Sir Benjamin sent him a message asking him not to let a question of money come between them. However, John was determined to go and he and his wife and their six surviving children, ranging in age from 14 years to two weeks, left Llanover. They sailed from Liverpool on the *Enoch Train* at the end of March and arrived in Boston five weeks later. They then went to Iowa where the men built handcarts to carry their possessions, as there were no wagons available.

They joined the handcart company led by Edmund Ellsworth. It took six months for them to reach Salt Lake City – six months of hardship and privation. Young William Powell was so thrilled to see their destination at last that he ran, pulling one of the family's handcarts with him. He was the first of the company to enter Salt Lake City, and that company was the first handcart

---

78   Mary Powell Sabin wrote the story of the Powell family.

company to reach there.

The Elders' promise to John was kept; he worked on the Temple for one day, then was taken ill, and died two weeks after their triumphant arrival in Salt Lake City.

A Typical Handcart Family

Image reproduced by kind permission of Neil B. Taylor

Lady Llanover [Lady Hall] was responsible for the survival of my ancestor John Powell. When no one else in the village would help him during an epidemic, she stood by him and his family and nursed him back to health. There are many hundreds, if not thousands, of his descendants in the U.S. who honor [sic] her name as well as that of her good husband Benjamin.

NEIL TAYLOR

According to Lord Palmerston,[79] Sir Benjamin had shown himself to be 'an able Manager and administrator' and he thought that the Queen[80] would find him a 'satisfactory Head of the Department of Works'[81] [formerly the Department of Woods and Forests]. Her Majesty agreed and Sir Benjamin was appointed Chief Commissioner of Works. The *New York Times*, on 3rd August

---

79   Henry John Temple, 1784-1865, 3rd Viscount Palmerston, Prime Minister 1855-8 and 1859-65

80   In a letter to Queen Victoria, dated July 1855

81   *THSC, Session 1964, Part I,* 'Lord Llanover (Big Ben) in London', Maxwell Fraser

1855 commented:

> *Sir Benjamin, who is a precise, well-looking, well-dressed gentleman, has some fluency as a public speaker, and is said to be a methodical man of business. He would gain nothing, in a pecuniary way, by stepping from the Board of Health to the office of the Woods and Forests, (the salary in each case being £2,000 per annum,) ... and although he might not have a seat in the Cabinet ... his own gain would be additional patronage ... and an additional claim on the Government for the Coronet, which, it is believed, he anxiously desires to obtain.*

He found his new department in a state of chaos and immediately set about clearing the backlog of work that had been allowed to accumulate by his predecessors.

Ever conscious of those less fortunate than himself, and anxious to better their lot, Sir Benjamin arranged to have the London parks open to the general public on a Sunday, the only spare time the working people had to relax and enjoy healthy surroundings. He requested money to make the gardens more accessible and attractive; tree-lined roads were constructed, flowerbeds dug and shrubs planted. There was much opposition to the plans for making the parks accessible to all, but the most serious opposition was to the idea of having bands play in the parks on Sundays. Sir Benjamin had gained the approval of Parliament and of the Queen and he was delighted at the initial success of his scheme; by the end of the season thousands of people had enjoyed the experience. However, when the bands began to play again at the start of the next season, in April 1856, the Sabbatarians began to campaign against them and the Prime Minister gave way under the pressure, in spite of the support Sir Benjamin's plan had from the Queen. Sir Benjamin, not willing to give in, made enquiries and found that it was only military bands that were banned; private bands would not be stopped from playing. The success of his idea must have brought him much satisfaction.

Some years earlier it had been decided that the Houses of Parliament, needing to be rebuilt after being almost completely destroyed by fire in 1834, would have 'a great clock, the best that could be made'.[82] For a long time the whole project had been held up by 'quarrelling and incompetence' but Sir Benjamin soon got to grips with the matter and arranged for the clock bell to be made at the foundry of Messrs. Warner and Sons, Stockton-on-Tees.

---

82   ibid

At last, on the 16th August 1856 the enormous bell was cast.[83] Weighing nearly sixteen tons, it was sounded for the first time on the 22nd August with a clapper of 7 cwt. Its note was E natural and the tone was considered to be 'very fine' by all who heard it. Its diameter was 9 feet 5 ½ inches and its height 7 feet 10 ½ inches and the inscription running round it was:

> *"Cast in the 20th year of the reign of her Majesty Queen Victoria, and in the year of our Lord 1856, from the design of Edmund Beckett Denison, Q.C.; Sir Benjamin Hall, Baronet, M.P., Chief Commissioner of Works".*

> *On the waist or middle of the bell are the Royal Arms, and the names of the founders and patentees of the mode of casting which has been adopted for it, "John Warner and Sons, Crescent Foundry, Cripplegate, London."[84]*

Moving Big Ben

Illustrated London News: Photograph John Weedy

From the foundry at Norton[85] the bell was taken by rail to West Hartlepool. Its huge size made it impossible for another train to pass, so it was moved on a Sunday when it had the track to itself. On the morning of the 21st October 1856 'The *Wave* was … safely delivered of her monster burden' which had been brought by sea to a wharf near Westminster. The bell was loaded onto a low truck drawn by sixteen horses and taken over Westminster Bridge to Palace-yard, Westminster. A large crowd gathered to watch as it was lifted from the truck and swung under a huge frame made especially for the purpose. There, at the foot of the Clock Tower, it was tested and pronounced free of cracks and flaws. The report in *The Times* is headed 'BIG BEN OF WESTMINSTER' and ends:

> *All bells, we believe, are christened before they begin to toll, and on this occasion it is proposed to call our king of bells "Big Ben," in honour of Sir Benjamin Hall, the President of the Board of Works, during whose tenure of office it was cast.*

83 The Whitechapel Bell Foundry web site.
84 *Illustrated London News*
85 Norton, near Stockton–on–Tees

A year later – disaster! The great bell cracked! The crack rose 'perpendicularly from the rim to rather more than half-way up the side.' Fortunately it had not been hoisted to the Tower because the quarter bells and the clock were not yet ready to be put in place. There was reason to hope that 'under the present Chief Commissioner [Sir Benjamin Hall]... the works will some day or other be brought to a conclusion.' Sir Benjamin must have been dismayed to hear that all his efforts to bring harmony to the discord between the 'scientific gentlemen' had come to this! He returned to London to 'personally inquire into all the circumstances of the case' and it was agreed that the bell should be recast using the metal from the original one. Due to 'the strongly expressed wish of the public, who were desirous of hearing its beautiful tone' the bell had been struck for a short period every Saturday but this was not thought to have caused the damage; it was considered fortunate that it had not been fixed in the Tower and the clock put in place.

The Times correspondent wrote :-

With respect to the chime of bells, Mr. Denison[86] *is of opinion that when they are finished, and if the same purity of tone can be got out of the "young Big Ben" as was obtained from "old Big Ben," the chime will be unequalled in the world.*

A very dramatic report of the breaking up of "Big Ben" was given in *The Times* on the 19th February 1858. The huge bell was lowered from its frame and its head sank into the earth 'so as to leave its mouth ... slightly inclined upwards, yawning like an enormous cavern.' An iron ball weighing twenty-four hundredweight was hoisted 'to a height of about 30 feet' then allowed 'to fall with all its weight upon poor Ben, who remained open-mouthed below as if gasping to receive his fate.' The 'death blow' came at 11.30 on the morning of Wednesday the 17th of February, when the heavy ball was dropped on 'the inside of "Ben's" sound bow, and incontinently, with a crazy bellow he yielded up the ghost – two pieces ... being knocked clean out of his side.' The breaking up continued rapidly and within a week all the pieces of metal had been carted off to the 'dingy foundry' of Messrs. Mears in a 'little back street in Whitechapel.' On examination it was found that 'speckiness prevailed almost throughout [Ben's] entire substance to a considerable extent'.

While the breaking up of 'old Big Ben' was taking place, Lord Palmerston's government fell and by the time the 'young Big Ben' had been cast, the new

---

86   Mr E. B. Denison, QC, later Lord Denison, designer of Big Ben

Prime Minister, the Earl of Derby,[87] had appointed Lord John Manners[88] as Chief Commissioner of Works. A question arose in the press – would the new bell retain its name of 'Big Ben' or would it be called after the new Chief Commissioner of Works, 'Big John'? By 14th May 1858 the new bell, of the same dimensions but not as heavy as its predecessor, had been hung and rung and Mr Denison was satisfied that its tone and manufacture were excellent. It was 'tastefully ornamented with gothic figures and tracery' but it did not have the name of the Commissioner of Works inscribed on it.[89]

When Sir Benjamin left office he no doubt felt that had done good, sound work. Having been re-elected by the voters of Marylebone in March 1858 he must have been confident that when his party was returned to power he would be given another administrative post. This, however, was not to be. Sir Benjamin, always loyal, could be relied upon not to make a fuss, so when Lord Palmerston was returned as Prime Minister, in June 1859, appointments went to those who might be troublesome if overlooked, and Sir Benjamin was 'fobbed off' with a title.[90] As Baron Llanover of Llanover and Abercarn, he took his seat in the House of Lords on 4th July 1859.

---

87   Edward George Geoffrey Smith Stanley, 1799-1869, 14th Earl of Derby
88   Lord John Manners, 1818-1906
89   *The Times*
90   *THSC, Session 1964, Part I*, 'Lord Llanover (Big Ben) in London', Maxwell Fraser

Chapter 4

Lord and Lady Llanover
(1859-1867)

And when she became Lady Llanover her affection for Wales and its institutions seems only to have gathered strength.[1]

You all know with what intensity, I may almost say passion, Lady Llanover has devoted herself to the interest of Wales ...[2]

The news of Sir Benjamin's elevation to the peerage had a mixed reception in the press. *The Sun* was very pleased for him saying, 'his patriotic and fearless career as a true reformer had long made him a favourite among the denizens of freedom'. He was praised for 'having done his duty admirably' as the Member for Marylebone, the largest and richest of the Metropolitan boroughs. As plain Mr Hall, the reporter wrote, he had been 'conspicuous among the patriot-reformers of the Welsh mountains ... the very life and soul of Reform in the dark days of ultra-Toryism.' He had been consistent in his conduct as a Member of Parliament and as a result he was made a baronet. When he was First Commissioner of Works he did more good for the metropolis than any of his predecessors had done over the previous thirty years.

> *Originally a thoroughbred and independent Radical, he gradually became fascinated by aristocratic associations, and gradually slid down the slippery slope of Whiggism, but chivalrously spurned its meanness.[3]*

Towards the end of June 1859 there was a large attendance at the Marylebone Vestry where Sir Benjamin gave his farewell address. The following resolution was proposed, seconded and unanimously accepted, amid much cheering:

> *That the congratulations of this vestry be offered to the Right Hon. Sir B. Hall, Bart., on his elevation to the House of Lords, and at the same time he be assured of the sense which this vestry entertains of the great ability and zeal with which he has devoted himself to all matters affecting the interests of the parish, and*

---

1   *The Western Mail,* after the death of Lady Llanover
2   *Transactions of the Royal National Eisteddfod, 1884*
3   *The Caledonian Mercury*

of the readiness of access and courteous attention which he has shown to all persons connected with it ... [4]

In his reply Lord Llanover thanked his listeners and said 'it was only due to them to state the real circumstances under which he left them.' It appears that when Lord Palmerston was forming the recent Government there were many claims to satisfy and Sir Benjamin, as he then was, was the first person his Lordship had sent for. It had been proposed to return him to the post of First Commissioner of Works, but without a seat in the Cabinet. If Sir Benjamin felt unable to return to that post without a seat in the Cabinet, there should be some public acknowledgement of his services, and so Lord Palmerston had recommended to the Queen 'that which her Majesty had been graciously pleased to confer on him.' Lord Palmerston had also hinted that there might be a time when the newly created Lord Llanover's services would be needed, should he feel inclined to give them. His Lordship concluded his speech to his former constituents by declaring that 'his services would ever be at their disposal.'

The North Wales Chronicle explained the title taken by Sir Benjamin:

Lord Llanofer's Coat of Arms

Illustrated London News: Photograph John Weedy

> *"Llan," signifying a consecrated place, dedicated to some particular saint ... and Llanover is the Church of St Gover. The penultimate is pronounced long, as in Dover, and not short, as in Hanover.*

The reporter goes on to mention the two wells in Kensington Gardens, St Agnes's Well and St Gover's Well, the latter having been erected and named by Sir Benjamin when he was First Commissioner of Works.

> *The water is considered a fine tonic, and is much resorted to by invalids, who are sent there by various members of the medical profession.*

The London correspondent of *The Belfast News-letter* was no fan of Lord Llanover! He quotes a 'caustic writer, now no more,' saying, 'the Radicals (hang the fellows) they have neither hearts nor heads.' In his opinion there were few finer specimens of a Radical than Lord Llanover, and as Sir Ben-

---

jamin Hall, MP, he was one of 'the trio of obstructives with whom Lord Palmerston had to deal when he succeeded to office in February last.' [The other two 'obstructives' were Mr V. Smith and Mr H. Labouchere.]

At the beginning of October Lord Llanover was 'at home', where he received the congratulations of his family, friends and tenants. The London correspondent of *The Belfast News-letter* was just as sarcastic in describing the occasion, although he had not been there but relied on the word of an 'eyewitness'. 'The liberality of the household arrangements at Llanover have … become a byword in the principality,' he wrote, and proceeded to quote the words of a 'local poet with more wit than charity' who had composed a verse about Llanover being a place 'whose hearth never blazes, whose chimneys never smoke, and where the stranger and the wayfarer see nothing but the front of the hall-door.' The correspondent continued by stating that, in spite of Lord Llanover's wealth and liberal views, it was said in the neighbourhood that he had done nothing to maintain the reputation of Welsh hospitality; it was said in Wales that he favoured Marylebone, while the people of Marylebone thought him too partial to Wales!

The mockery continued in the description of the celebration; 'Lord Llanover himself condescended to be present'; 'a cold dinner with plenty of cold water to wash it down was provided'; 'no beverage more generous than tea or coffee was dispensed'; 'a more absurd attempt at a revival of the feudal system was never witnessed'. Apparently the applause was delirious

The Hall of Llanover House

when his Lordship attributed his success to the assistance of his wife, and then 'several persons (who had been observed to consult occasionally short black bottles called in the vernacular "cuddachs"[5]) were carried off by their friends, and laid under the trees …'

The Liverpool Mercury and *The Bristol Mercury* were kinder, reporting that Lord Llanover's neighbours, tenants and friends in Glamorganshire and

---

5   Possibly from 'cudd' – hidden, concealed

Monmouthshire had received the news of his peerage 'with great satisfaction' and had congratulated him.

As the weather was unfavourable on the day they were 'at home', Lord and Lady Llanover received their visitors in 'the splendid hall of the mansion … in something like feudal pomp and state.'[6]

His Lordship took the opportunity to mention his support of the temperance movement, saying that although it had been the subject of 'many a rude joke and idle jest' it was of great benefit then and would be in the future.

All his workmen had embraced temperance voluntarily, and for several years his harvests had been got in without the consumption of any strong drink. The money had been received by the workmen's wives, and spent in useful purposes instead of being squandered in public houses.[7]

A week later *The Manchester Times* was asking, 'What is the use of a Radical Peer? Why was Sir Benjamin Hall made a peer? Of what value is Lord Llanover in the House of Lords?' The paper claimed that as Lord Llanover himself could not answer satisfactorily, no-one else could be expected to do so.

Had Lord Palmerston desired to exhibit his contempt for the House of Lords as an element in the British constitution he could scarcely have hit upon an expedient more likely to succeed … No-one grudges his peerage to Lord Brougham,[8] but what, we ask, had Sir Benjamin Hall done that he should be pensioned off to the House of Lords?

The writer thought it a possibility that in time Lord Llanover might prove that he possessed some excellent qualities that were not apparent when he was First Commissioner of Works!

Perhaps the elegant repose of the Lords may be favourable to the development of profound political thought, and the commonplace Radical of the Commons may become a shining light in the Upper House … we shall watch the career of the Radical baron with considerable interest.

Just when Lord Llanover was celebrating 'in sparkling cups of pure spring water his election to the peerage' the *Belfast News-letter* seemed to take a perverse pleasure in reporting that the 'new' Big Ben had cracked!

---

6   *The Bristol Mercury*
7   *The Liverpool Mercury*
8   Lord Brougham, 1778-1868, designer of the brougham carriage

Lord Llanover's prospects of handing down his name to a remote Cockney Pos-
terity are now for ever crushed, and, with the fracture of Big Ben, the proba-
bility is that the noble lord himself will sink into oblivion unwept, unhonoured,
and unchimed.

The unfortunate Henry Fitzroy[9] was First Commissioner of Works then, and no doubt was expected to deal with the problem. However, he left the job in February 1860, his successor being the Hon. William Cowper.

At this time there was much discussion about the Church in Wales, and the practice of appointing non-Welsh speaking clergymen to Welsh parishes. Lord Llanover had constantly opposed this practice 'and whether it arose from religious motives or personal feeling, he made more than one bishop wince under his powerful pen.' Those attending colleges and seminaries to prepare for holy orders were able to study many 'learned languages' and it came as a surprise to some that the study of Welsh, a living language, was not considered important. Reference was made to the college at Lampeter, established after much trouble, where Welsh could be studied but...

The tardiness in settling such an institution and the perfect indifference shown
towards the mother tongue of the ancient Britons are unworthy proofs of Saxon
antagonism to the ancient race.

It was thought 'a striking inconsistency' that much effort and expense was expended in instructing missionaries in the languages of remote places, but apparently no thought given to the Celtic languages.

The day may come when some of those dialects will be extinct, and when the
last person who has used it as his mother tongue quits the thread of this life,
an outcry may be raised, as was the case of the Cornish, which was lost when
Dolly Pentraeth breathed her last – the sole depositary of that interesting lan-
guage.[10]

There was concern too about 'the destruction of the ... shrubberies in the Parks.'[11] An 'indignant eyewitness' of this destruction complained that after considerable cost in time, effort and money spent during Lord Llanover's time as First Commissioner of Works, it should all be swept away at a moment's notice, and with no explanation. The plants had just become established and were thriving, and the public approved of Lord Llanover's scheme

---

9   Henry Fitzroy, First Commissioner of Works, June 1859-February 1860
10 James Logan in *Lloyd's Weekly Newspaper*
11 Andrew Agnew in *The Times*

and a lively discussion followed in *The Times*. According to 'A Lover of Flowers' in a letter to the Editor, people had come to appreciate the 'charming variety of flowers' and as far as the writer knew, they had 'so far civilised the denizens of our lanes and alleys that no poor ragged urchin has ever ... been convicted of stealing or destroying a single flower.'

'A Frequenter of the Parks' wanted to know why all the trees and shrubs had been uprooted, since the improvements made by Lord Llanover when First Commissioner of Works 'were a delight to every Londoner and the admiration of every foreigner.' Identifying himself only as 'P' another wrote to ask why flowers had been planted there in the first place! To expect flowers to thrive under the shade of established trees, whose roots took all the nourishment from the soil, 'proved that the projector of such a scheme was a very ignorant gardener.'

J. Mann, Superintendent of St James's, Green and Hyde Parks, and Kensington Gardens, responded to these letters as he was 'anxious to remove the misapprehensions' regarding his instructions, and he gave 'the facts.'

- When Lord Llanover was First Commissioner deciduous and ever green shrubs had been planted, together with a number of young trees, which, when ready, would be transplanted in other parts of the Park. Some annuals had been planted 'here and there'.

- During Lord John Manners'[12] time in office numerous flowers had been planted, and since then verbenas, geraniums etc. had been added.

- The shrubs did not thrive, and there were many objections to the mixture of flowers and shrubs, so it had been decided to remove the shrubs. Mr Mann had been instructed to replace them with flowering plants, to be put in the ground in the Spring.

- The only trees to have been removed were those planted for nursery purpose. In response to Mr Mann's letter, 'A Londoner' suggested that if it were true that the shrubs and trees did not thrive, then the responsibility for their failure rested on Mr Mann's shoulders, as he was the Superintendent of the Parks! He also mentioned an assertion by another letter-writer 'that the trees and shrubs were removed to please certain persons in Park Lane.'

---

12 Lord John Manners, First Commissioner of Works, February 1858-June 1859

By the 9th December deputations from Marylebone and Paddington visited Lord Palmerston, who, until then, knew nothing of the matter. The various resolutions were read to him:

- The public were happy at the results of Sir Benjamin's improvements but now they were 'deprived of a useful and elegant sort of recreation'

- Since Sir Benjamin had left office the shrubs had been 'shamefully neglected'

- There was a feeling that the rights of working class people had been undermined by 'the selfishness of a class, between whom and the labouring population goodwill should prevail'

- Sir Benjamin carried out the work 'with right good will' and had the approval of the Queen, who 'unhesitatingly assigned to him … a large portion of land, near Kew Palace, to be used as a nursery'

- He was asked to remove the trees as they had become 'an eyesore to some inhabitants of Park-lane, who imagined that they would ob-struct their view'. Sir Benjamin, of course, refused to do so, as did his successor, Lord John Manners.

It was thought that with 'the illness of the present First Commissioner, Henry Fitzroy, the administration of the office had been induced to comply with this unreasonable request'. Naturally the Office of Works denied any such thing! The Prime Minister promised to 'make it his business to inquire into it, and see what was best to be done.'

A few days later a severe frost set in and temperatures fell well below freezing point. Hundreds of people lined the lakesides watching the skaters and enjoying the sight of their mishaps! St James's Park was the most popular with the skaters since, as part of Lord Llanover's improvements, the lake had been lined with concrete and the depth of water made a uniform three to four feet; thus 'no immediate danger was to be apprehended.' For several days skaters continued to risk cuts and bruises, and possibly an icy plunge should the ice give way. Fortunately the Royal Humane Society employed people who, wearing cork jackets and carrying ropes, warned the public of the dan-gers. On one day there were said to be over 4000 skaters in Regent's Park and 6000 on the Serpentine. Although many received cuts and bruises, and one poor lad broke his arm, there were no fatalities. This was mainly thanks to 'the exertions of the persons employed by the Royal Humane Society, who, to guard against all contingencies, had been doubled in number.'[13]

Mr Spurgeon,[14] the celebrated preacher, was in the Abercarn area at the beginning of June 1860, where he preached to a crowd of at least 20,000 in a field belonging to a Mr Brown.[15] Among those present were many of the gentry of the county, including the Lord Lieutenant[16] and his wife, Lord and Lady Tredegar and family and Lord and Lady Llanover and family. Before the service began Mr Spurgeon was told it might be advisable for the people to make way for the carriages-and-four of the gentry. He replied that he was not there to preach to horses, but to men and that a carriage and four horses would take up the space of fifty people; so, no, the carriages and horses must stay where they were!

After the service the Lord Lieutenant invited Mr Spurgeon to Pontypool, but that gentleman could not accept as he was fully engaged for the next two years! The Preacher was complaining of tiredness, 'brought on, no doubt, by his indefatigable zeal.'[17] Over the previous seven years he had preached an average of ten sermons a week to very large congregations, but in spite of his physical and mental weariness he journeyed to the Continent where he continued his tour.

Early in 1860 Mr Henry Stone, who was well known in sporting circles in Bath, took action against Lord Llanover to recover damages for slander, 'it being alleged that the defendant [Lord Llanover] had charged the plaintiff [Mr Stone] with the commission of an unnatural offence.'[18]

Mr Stone was a young, married man, a former army officer who had inherited a small fortune on the death of his father. Six years earlier he had begun to suffer from an unpleasant complaint, and his condition worsened until his medical advisors told him he should not be left alone; he suffered from severe haemorrhaging, which sometimes resulted in dizzy spells and faintness. As the young man was very interested in horses and horse racing he spent a lot of time away from home and the security of his wife's presence, so on those occasions a man-servant would sleep in the same room, or one adjoining. On one occasion it was necessary for him to remain at his training

---

13 *The Times*

14 Charles Haddon Spurgeon, 1834–1892

15 *The Leeds Mercury*

16 Capel Hanbury Leigh, 1776–1861. Died from accidental poisoning

17 *The Leeds Mercury*

18 *The Bristol Mercury*

stable, where the only place for him to stay was his farrier's 'hovel', and, in case of emergency, his groom had to sleep in the same room.

Due to his illness Mr Stone was eventually forced to give up the excitement of horse racing and he disposed of the training stables. Following this he received a letter supposedly written by the farrier's wife, suggesting his conduct while there had been 'disgusting', and that she was willing to accept money from him to ensure her silence. On receiving legal advice to ignore the accusation, Mr Stone did just that, only for the matter to come to the fore again in a letter he received from Father Thompson, a 'Romish priest (Mr. Stone being a Roman Catholic).' Some gentlemen looked into the matter, and, finding no truth in the rumours, continued to associate with him. Mr Stone's club also made enquiries and found there to be no truth in the allegations.

The woman who wrote the damaging letter was about to be prosecuted, on the advice of Mr Stone's London solicitor, when the matter was dropped, and she stated on oath that her letter was 'utterly false.' Mr Stone thought that was the end of the matter, but to his dismay the 'unpleasant charges [were] again called to light' when he moved to Monmouthshire in 1859. He traced the rumours to Lord Llanover 'who he found had shown a paper to several persons imputing offensive charges to the plaintiff.'

Lord Llanover's brother, Richard Crawshay Hall, lived near Bath, where the rumours regarding Mr Stone were rife. In July 1858 he had written to Sir Benjamin, as he then was, about these rumours, because he had heard that Mr Stone was moving to the Llanover area. After reading the letter Sir Benjamin had torn it up 'into very small pieces, in order that no parts might be put together' and told no one of its content. A year later, when just about to return to Llanover from London, he heard that Mr Stone had indeed taken an estate in Monmouthshire, situated between Llanover and the home of his daughter and son-in-law at Llanarth. He checked with his brother in Bath, who replied that there had been an enquiry, the result of which had been unsatisfactory. Concerned lest his family become embroiled in a scandal, Lord Llanover wrote to John Herbert, his son-in-law, asking him to make enquiries about Mr Stone. Later he received another letter regarding Mr Stone from his brother in Bath, which he copied and sent to Mr Herbert, asking that it be returned, which it was, after Mr Herbert had made a copy for himself. This copy was 'taken away from his house … by unfair means' and reached the hands of Mr Stone. The action for libel was based on the contents of this letter as it reflected on the character of Mr Stone.

Sir F. Kelly, acting for Mr Stone, was 'perfectly convinced ... of the entire innocence of [his] client' but admitted that Mr Stone's behaviour had been stupid and that he had put himself in a position 'in which no one could be accused of rashness or injustice for entertaining suspicions of the most serious and painful nature.'[19] He also understood Lord Llanover's position. Having several 'near and dear relatives' living in the area, just a short distance from Mr Stone's residence, his Lordship could not ignore the rumours 'which undoubtedly prevailed.'

The proceedings eventually concluded with Lord Llanover being vindicated for his actions and Mr Stone declaring that he disclaimed 'all desire to recover damages' and his only wish was to leave the court with his character clear. Mr Justice Hill must have breathed a sigh of relief. 'I am very glad for the sake of the public,' he said, 'that this painful case has terminated.' Sadly, 'a lasting stigma rested on Mr Stone'[20] and the whole episode left 'a sad impression on the families of Scrope[21] and Herbert.' Some blamed Lady Llanover who was 'jealous of Kathleen Stone because her beauty was so superior to that of her daughter Mrs Herbert ...'

While her husband was busy with his various duties and problems, Lady Llanover was busy with her own projects, one of which was the enormous task of editing the correspondence of her mother's great aunt, Mrs Delany. In October 1860 *Trewman's Exeter Flying Post* declared that the book world was showing 'decided signs of animation.'

> *... all the peerage seems rushing into print. ... and Lady Llanover will add to her pin-money (I hope) by the proceeds of 'The Autobiography of Mary Granville afterwards Mrs. Delany.'*

The first three volumes of this impressive work were completed by the middle of December, 1860, when it was advertised as a new work 'now ready.' There were 600 pages in each volume with 'numerous fine Engravings from original oil paintings, Miniatures and Enamels by Zincke, and some from the exquisite Portland enamels.' The cost of the three volumes was forty-two shillings.[22] *The Times* reported that ...

> *The best is yet to come, the last eight-and-twenty years of [Mrs Delany's] life, when age had ennobled her, and when she moved about the world in it, but not*

19 *The Times*
20 *Recollections of a Northumbrian Lady, 1815-1866*, Memoirs of Barbara Tasburgh Charlton
21 Simon Thomas Scrope/Scroope married Jane Mary Jones, daughter of John Jones of Llanarth, in 1821
22 *The Examiner*

of it. She had known everybody, and could talk to the rising generations of innumerable persons, now existing but in name.

By December the following year the whole work was finished; the final three volumes were available 'immediately'[23] – at a cost of fifty shillings!

Carl Bunsen

Towards the end of his life, Lady Llanover's brother-in-law, Baron Bunsen, said to her 'I have always felt for you, and with you, more than you ever knew.'[24] As the year 1860 was nearing its close Baron Bunsen became seriously ill and there was little hope of recovery. He died in Bonn in November and his funeral, on the 1st December, was attended by friends and family, including Lord and Lady Llanover. According to a newspaper report[25] his and his family's connections through marriage with this country had 'made him almost one of ourselves,' but 'he was always a true German, ponderous, learned, and unreadable.' His King had made him a diplomat 'when his real tastes and talents qualified him for the professor's chair.' With his death, Lady Llanover lost not just a dear brother-in-law, but someone who understood and supported her endeavours on behalf of her beloved Wales.

Despite the demise of the Abergavenny Cymreigyddion Society in 1854, Lady Llanover maintained her interest in and her support of eisteddfodau. For instance, she offered a prize of £3 at the 1858 Llangollen Eisteddfod, 'to the day labourer (whose weekly wages do not exceed one pound) with the greatest number of children at the Eisteddfod able to read and write in Welsh.' There was just one competitor – Thomas Jones of Brynmelyn, Trevor. He had

---

23   ibid
24   *A Memoir of Baron Bunsen*
25   *Trewman's Exeter Flying Post*

five of his children with him, and a certificate showing that the sixth child was ill![26]

Thomas Griffiths, *Gruffydd*, the Llanover harper, was among the performers at various eisteddfodau. At the evening concert before the Denbigh National Eisteddfod in August 1860 he played 'an admirable solo on the harp, and was rapturously applauded.'[27] At the same Eisteddfod Mrs Manuel, mother of those remarkable boys who had astounded *Carnhuanawc* and others many years earlier, was awarded a prize for her essay on 'Female Education'. The harp competition was judged by Lady Willoughby de Broke, who awarded the prize to Llewelyn Williams[28] of Monmouthshire.

The National Eisteddfod at Conway in 1861 was looked forward to with great anticipation. The *North Wales Chronicle* announced that not only would 'a great number of the aristocracy, clergy, and literati' be attending, but they were to be honoured by the presence of none other than 'that eminent patron of Welsh literature,' Lady Llanover. The writer thought that everything had been arranged admirably, and he was confident that the meeting would be a success. Various works of art were to be displayed in the banqueting hall of the castle, and among the musicians appearing were Miss Sarah Edith Wynne (*Eos Cymru*),[29] Mr Ellis Roberts (*Eos Meirion*),[30] Mr T. D. Morris, 'the celebrated harpist of Bangor',[31] and *Llew Llwyfo*, Lewis William Lewis,[32] of Anglesey.

David Williams, *Morgrygun*, the woollen manufacturer who had emigrated to Australia in 1841, prospered in his new life; his son Josiah had died on the voyage, but, once settled in Australia, he and his wife had more sons – David Evan, Taliesin and Ivor Josiah. In 1861 he brought the boys back to Britain to see the land of their forebears. When the others returned to Australia David Evan stayed behind to attend college, and on Christmas Eve the young man travelled to Llanover to pay his respects to Lord and Lady Llanover.

I asked one of the footmen that I wanted to [see] her Ladyship then I was asked what would he tell her who I was which I replied, David Williams late from Australia, and then he replied with a grunt from his nose and off he went …

---

26 I am grateful to Michael Freeman former Curator, Ceredigion Museum, for this snippet.

27 *The Musical World*

28 Probably the son of Zephaniah Williams, the chartist

29 Sarah Edith Wynne, 1842-1897, made her first London appearance in 1862

30 Ellis Roberts, *Eos Meirion*, 1819-1873, harper to the Prince of Wales

31 Possibly Thomas Morris, 1827-1868, of Rhuthun and Bangor

32 Lewis William Lewis, 1831-1901, poet, novelist, journalist and raconteur

The young man had to wait a few hours in the housekeeper's room before he was summoned. While he was waiting he was given dinner and had the company of Mr Rees, Lady Llanover's scripture reader. When he eventually met her Ladyship he was surprised at her plain dress and manner. Her first words to the young man were, 'How is your father, I heard you were in Normal College.[33]' When asked what he intended to be the young man replied, 'a farmer My Lady.'

1862 Sketch of Lady Llanover
Western Mail: Photograph Moira Harry

Did [your father] send you home only to get schooling, no My Lady it was more for to see the country than anything else, and so forth and then I had it right and left from her ... [34]

Her Ladyship thought it was ridiculous to send a boy to school to be 'nothing else than a farmer.' David should be behind the plough every day from dawn to dusk; a farmer only needed 'to read and write a legible hand and cast the first 4 rules of arithmetic.' Then she began to berate the poor fellow about his father; why did he leave a comfortable home to go to an 'uncivilised country, out of the spread of the gospel and rearing his children in ignorance'; he had been doing well at his trade and her Ladyship still had 'as good a piece of flannel now as was ever weaved in Wales.' He had a good livelihood here, and 'now he has lost his wife he has lost everything.' Eventually the scolding ended and David was able to escape and go out walking in the beautiful countryside with Mr Rees.

After supper on Christmas Eve everybody was busy dressing candlesticks with coloured paper in readiness for the *Plygain*, the early service, on Christmas morning.

---

33 Probably Swansea Normal College
34 The diary of David Williams. My thanks to Ann Hall and Paul Williams

Although late to bed they were all stirring by half-past five the following morning and 'rallied out into the darkness' with their decorated candles and followed the path to the church. David Williams had been 'requested' to attend the service by her Ladyship, so he left his lodging in the village very early. The moon was shining on the frost-covered ground and the sight of the candles approaching the Church, although beautiful, reminded David of corpse candles.[35] Lady Llanover also went down the path carrying her lighted candle.

After the service it was back for breakfast. Then began the preparations for the dinner for the tenants and workmen. About two hundred were served, in two sittings, with the tables …

'very nicely laid out without a drop of intoxicating drinks … a nice site [sic] it was too, big joints and roast meat … with mutton, veal and pork etc. with an addition of vegetable, ginger pop, lemonade and harmless wine …'

The walls were bedecked with green leaves and branches, and a variety of flags old and new. On one of the flags, which had been made by the servants, was written '*Llanover dros byth* (Llanover for ever)'; on another '*Cysured Duw ein Brenhines* (God Comfort our Queen)'. Lord and Lady Llanover checked the preparations to see that everything was done to their satisfaction. Everyone then set to with a will, but in spite of their hearty appetites there was some food remaining 'and the most of them pocketed the mince pies.'

After everything was cleared away preparations began for the evening's entertainment, which started with *Gruffydd*, the harper, playing a tune on the **English** harp! This amused David, to see him play a tune 'with tight strings'. There were speeches, singing and poetry readings but there was no dancing due to the recent death of Prince Albert.[36] The party ended at midnight, and David thought it was the happiest Christmas Day of his life.

He spent a few more days at Llanover and was very impressed. The windows of the *Llys* were 'cut so beautiful fine and the frame of the windows was like thread.' In the hall there were 'beautiful models of Italian architecure [sic] of 4 or 5 storys [sic]', and outside was an impressive rhododendron 'whose diameter was 30 yards and is reckoned amongst one of the largest of its kind in the world.' The garden was neat and clean with a fountain in the middle of a small pond and an island, reached by a bridge from the side, in

---

35 A luminous appearance, resembling the flame of a candle, sometimes seen in churchyards and other damp places, superstitiously regarded as portending death. *The Free Dictionary* online
36 Prince Albert, 1819-14th December 1861

the middle of a large pond. He toured the kitchen garden and the hot houses, where he was surprised to see oranges growing, and he remarked that 'everything was put to the utmost advantage and persons looking after the place and seeing that everything was in its proper place.' He went to *Tŷ Uchaf* where, depending on the weather, fires were lit in 'the principal parlours twice or three times a week.' The place was kept very clean and the floorboards were so highly polished that they posed a threat to the unwary!

On New Year's Day there was a supper for about forty people, followed by singing, dancing and games. *Gruffydd* opened the evening's entertainment, this time playing on the **Welsh** harp 'with the treble strings.' Everyone had a happy time and made up for the lack of dancing at Christmas. The evening ended about 11.30 and David returned to his lodgings in the village, where a sulky-looking landlady told him she was on the point of locking him out!

The following day the young man saw more of the estate. In the stables there were 'some splendid horses and mares' all of which were in immaculate condition, and everything was clean and well organised. After he was shown the various carriages he went to the laundry 'which was laid out to the utmost advantage'. In the middle was a boiler that supplied warm water to the wash tubs, which were fixed to the wall, and there were places for mangling, for ironing, for airing clothes and for drying feathers.

Welsh Triple Harp won by
Mrs Gruffydd Richards, Llandovery 1872
Thanks to Keith Floyd: Photograph Chris Barlow

On his last day David was taken to Lord Llanover's farm, which was laid out differently from other farms in the area. There were various types of ploughs and harrows, and a mowing machine, the first that David had ever seen. There were tools 'for everything that was required on a respectable farm.'

David left Llanover on the 4th January and began his journey back to Pontarddulais. Mrs Williams, the housekeeper, made certain he did not go empty handed and sent a servant after him with some mince pies and oranges, for which he was very grateful.

In September 1861, Margaret Davies,[37] the 19 year-old daughter of William Davies, agent to Lord Mostyn, went to Llanover, and stayed for a year. During that time she had various duties including time spent in the kitchens and the workroom and acting as an assistant secretary to Lady Llanover. She recorded her impressions in a diary, which gives an insight into the customs of the day.

Margaret and her father travelled to Llanover by train, a journey she enjoyed, admiring the countryside through which they passed. On arrival at Abergavenny they hired a hackney carriage to take them to Llanover, and entering the park through the Porth Mawr, she was most amused to see the

Porth Mawr

paths being brushed by women wearing 'hats and bobtails, and stuff aprons, etc.'

Later she realised that all the servants wore the same, and all spoke in

---

37   Margaret Davies, 1841-1935, m. Rev. J. Mostyn Jones in 1881

Welsh. The gardens delighted her; they were immaculate with the grass soft and smooth and the broad, red-gravelled paths neatly swept and free from weeds.

There was also a large fountain playing and splashing up its waters, and again further on was a large lake with swans, geese and ducks of all kinds on it, who lodged on the islands in it.

There were flowers and shrubs of many varieties, nine crystal springs 'forming the holy Fountain of Gofer, the hermit, which gave the name to Llanover', and eight glasshouses where vines and pineapples grew.

The young woman soon met some of the people with whom she was to work and socialise during the next few months – Mrs Davies, lady's maid, Thomas Griffiths, the harper, and a very shy young man named Theophilus Rees who, that very day, had been appointed Lady Llanover's Scripture Reader.

It was two days later, when she had already spent most of the day in the workroom, that Lady Llanover finally sent for her. Another few minutes went by before her Ladyship entered the room where Margaret was waiting. She was rather different from Margaret's mental image of her!

She had on a stuff skirt tucked up all around, a black velvet jacket, a puce bow attached to her collar, no cap as I had anticipated, black silk stockings and little shoes with ribbon bows.[38]

Lady Llanover's conversation was also unexpected. Kindly but firmly stating her 'accustomed rules' her Ladyship scrutinised Margaret carefully and then went on to speak of other things, some of which moved Margaret to tears.

On their first Sunday in Llanover Margaret and her father attended Capel Ed in the morning and Llanover Chapel 'in the Pentre' in the evening. In between they attended the Welsh service in the Church, which was full as all the servants of the *Llys* were there. In her diary Margaret commented on the high hats, and mentioned that Lady Llanover always wore hers on Sunday. After the evening service in the village chapel the Llanover choir gathered in the House and practised their singing. Then, after supper, they went to the gallery where they impressed Margaret with their renderings of three or four beautiful hymns, the magnificent sound of their voices being especially

---

38 *Country Quest* 'Lady Below Stairs' ed. David Thomas

effective in the 'stillness that reigned all about.' At 10 o'clock, a bell rang and her Ladyship and all the house servants assembled in the front hall where Lady Llanover read Evening Prayers. So began Margaret's year at Llanover.

In November she, with Mrs Manuel and Mr Rees,[39] began to collect the names of the poor and to note what they needed and she was shocked to see such poverty. By the end of the month the goods were ready to be packed and labelled; Margaret thought that they were all like 'counter-jumpers'. Each person was called in by Mr Rees and shown into the servants' hall by Elizabeth Manuel. Mrs Manuel then called his or her name and Margaret had the task of finding the right bundle, which she gave to Lady Llanover who spoke to each person in Welsh. The *plant bach Llanarth*[40] were there also, and they helped their grandmother to distribute the parcels to the needy people, who were dressed in 'the Welsh style'. It seemed to Margaret that this was the first time those clothes had been worn since 'the last time they came for their clothing'. The whole event took two days!

Just before Christmas the young woman was busy once more making and distributing clothing to over a hundred people. Then came the Christmas

Lord Llanover
Image reproduced by kind permission
of Gwent Archives

preparations – making bunting and collecting holly and mistletoe to decorate the servants' hall, which 'really looked beautiful.' On Christmas morning she went with the others to the church for the *Plygain* and afterwards helped to prepare the dinner for the tenants and workmen. She reports in her diary that they 'were very merry all the next days.'

In January Margaret helped with the *Mari Lwyd*.[41] To attract Lord Llanover's attention 'to the play that was going on outside'[42] the harpers played outside the library window. Margaret found it very amusing, as she had never before heard of such a thing. [In spite of Mrs Lucy, in her memoirs, giving the impression that

---

39   Theophilus Rees, Lady Llanover's Scripture Reader
40   The little children of Llanarth – as Lady Llanover referred to her grandchildren
41   *Mari Lwyd* – lit. Grey Mary. A horse's skull draped with a sheet and adorned with ribbons
42   The Diary of Margaret Davies

his Lordship was rather disagreeable, it is not difficult to picture that genial gentleman enjoying the incident and smiling at hearing the sweet strains of the revered old instrument.]

There was a dinner party in February when Lord and Lady Tredegar and Miss Morgan were among the guests, and later in the month there was the excitement for Margaret Davies and Elizabeth Manuel of helping Miss Waddington to dress for the Hunt Ball in Abergavenny. Then they went to the gallery overlooking the front hall to watch the company gather to await their carriages.

Soon it was the 1st of March, St David's Day, but the usual practice of the schoolchildren coming to be examined by her Ladyship did not occur as she was not well on that occasion.

On the 19th of May about twenty people, including Margaret Davies, went to the Eisteddfod at Brynmawr, all wearing Welsh costume, and Elizabeth Manuel and herself wearing red cloaks. They all presented themselves to Lady Llanover before setting out and she pronounced herself very pleased with them. They took their places on the coach about eight in the morning, and as they moved away they cheered her Ladyship who had come to see them off. They sang Welsh songs on the journey and arrived in Brynmawr after about two hours.

At the Eisteddfod Margaret, Mrs Manuel and Mrs Edwards[43] were called upon to award some of the prizes, 'in fact all the rest did', and although the party from Llanover had planned to leave early in the evening they 'could not prevail upon the people to let [them] leave the stage.' So, in the dark, with the 'postilions not over sober' they descended some very steep hills. This made Margaret rather nervous but she was sitting next to Mr Rees who had the responsibility of 'the dragging of the wheel',[44] and they arrived back at Llanover a little after midnight 'without anything uncomfortable having happened.'

Lady Llanover was ill at this time and in the middle of March went to Tenby to recuperate, taking young Margaret and a Miss Lucas with her. Also spending time in the town were the Herberts of Llanarth, the Misses Williams of Aberpergwm and Sir John Gardner Wilkinson and his wife, the former Caroline Catherine Lucas. Lady Wilkinson had been a much-loved companion

43   It is not known who Mrs Edwards was
44   Applying the brake?

of Lady Llanover in the 1850s and she and Sir John were married at Llanover in 1856. The Miss Lucas in the Tenby party was probably Minna, Mary Elizabeth Lucas, who later, at Llanover, married William Watkins.[45] Lady Llanover was very fond of the Lucas girls, and yet another sister followed Minna as her companion.

The months must have flown by for Margaret, busy as she was, and soon it was time to say goodbye. Lady Llanover was due to go to London at the end of September and would not be back before Margaret returned to North Wales, so she sent for the young woman and spoke to her at length. She told her she had been 'a very good girl' and that she was sorry the girl was leaving. She hoped that Margaret would write to her, and told her she would be welcome at Llanover any time she wished to visit. Then 'with a shake of the hand the interview was over.'

Back home in North Wales Margaret loved to surprise her friends by quietly slipping away from their company and returning dressed in the Welsh costume as she wore it in Llanover; 'sugar loaf hat with a leek in it, a flannel dress (Llanover Christmas gift), a stuff apron and a shoulder shawl.' To add to their amusement she adopted a South Walian accent when she spoke to them.

One of Lady Llanover's protégées at this time was Elizabeth [Betha] Johnes, the younger daughter of Judge John Johnes of Dolaucothi. Her mother had died when Betha was about seven years old, and it was Lady Llanover who 'brought her out' in Society. The young woman became Lady Llanover's 'most intimate and prolific correspondent.' Lord Llanover's nephew, Arthur Berrington[46] was his uncle's private secretary for a while, and poor Betha fell deeply in love with him. Lady Llanover did her best to make a match between them, practically ordering Arthur to marry Betha and 'badgering him to an extent that no self-respecting man could endure.'[47] The resulting family quarrel was very bitter, and the previous affectionate relationship was never fully restored. Arthur subsequently married his late wife's sister, and Betha, whose emotions were very disturbed, remained a spinster for many years. Eventually, in 1882, she married Sir James Hills, VC,[48] and they lived happily at

---

45   William Watkins, son of Jeffrey Watkins of Llandovery, a tradesman
46   Arthur Berrington, son of Jenkin Davies Berrington the Younger, 1801-1885 and Charlotte Hall;
     m. i) Frances Heneage Lane in 1853; ii) Ada Barbara Lane
47   *THSC* 'Lady Llanover and Her Circle', Maxwell Fraser
48   Lieut-General Sir James Hills-Johnes, 1833-1919, won the VC during the Indian Mutiny, 9 July 1857

Dolaucothi with Charlotte,[49] Betha's widowed sister. Sir James changed his name by royal licence to Hills-Johnes.

Another who became part of the Llanover circle in the 1860s was Geraldine Jewsbury, the Victorian novelist. She loved the legends of Wales and the wild scenery around Llanover, and became fond of Lady Llanover, not simply because she was a ' "great lady" but also [because she] had time for literary interests.'[50] A passionate, emotional and demanding woman, she sometimes tried the patience of Lady Llanover, who, in a letter to Betha, wrote 'I have been *truly annoyed* at the good (but flighty) Jewsbury ... '[51] In her later years Geraldine began to suffer from the effects of a tumour. She was at Llanover when this first became apparent, and although she was never an easy visitor, she was made welcome during the last few winters of her life and was nursed devotedly by Lady Llanover.

Sir James Hills-Johnes VC
Image reproduced by kind permission
of Steven John

Yet of all the hundreds of letters written by Miss Jewsbury which survive, some of which were written whilst staying at Llanover, not a single one makes any mention of her host and hostess.[52]

William Jones of Clytha, Monmouthshire, was an uncle of John Herbert, Lord Llanover's son-in-law. In February 1862 William Jones made a public announcement that he had changed his surname to Herbert, and from then on he would be known as William Herbert of Clytha. His son, who wished to have a commission in the Royal Monmouth Militia, asked the Lord Lieutenant of the county, Lord Llanover, to submit his name for the Queen's approval, using the name Herbert. His Lordship knew it was not against any

---

49 Charlotte, widow of Captain Cookman of Enniscorthy, Ireland
50 Susanne Howe, biographer, in *THSC* 'Lady Llanover and Her Circle', Maxwell Fraser
51 In a letter dated 12th October 1864, *THSC* 'Lady Llanover and Her Circle', Maxwell Fraser
52 *THSC* 'Lady Llanover and Her Circle', Maxwell Fraser

law to use a different surname, but refused to put forward the assumed name as 'it would be an infringement on the Queen's prerogative ... to submit a name assumed without the Royal license [sic].'[53] William Jones then applied to the clerk of the Crown for a writ enabling him to serve as a justice of the peace for the county, in the name of Herbert. As his name in the Commission of the Peace was Jones, his application was refused.

Later that year a newspaper published a statement saying that the Lord Chancellor had agreed to Mr Jones's change of name. Lord Llanover, believing the statement to be untrue, wrote to the Lord Chancellor to clarify the matter. The reply stated that the Lord Chancellor 'had not recognised Mr. Jones as entitled to be called Herbert', but when he had obtained the Royal licence, he would order the change to be made in the Commission of the Peace.

> ... with characteristic disregard of courtesy and noticeable ignorance of law, [the Lord Chancellor] directs his secretary to inform the Lord Lieutenant that he has not recognised the right of Mr. Jones to assume the name of Herbert, and will not do so until Mr. Jones has obtained the royal license [sic] to bear that name.[54]

At that time the Commission of Sewers for Monmouthshire was about to end, and a petition was raised for a new Commission to be formed. Mr Jones's name appeared in the old Commission, and in spite of the refusal to acknowledge his use of the name Herbert, the clerk was ordered to alter Jones to Herbert on the list to be submitted. It was necessary for the petition to be signed by the Lord Lieutenant, which he did, having satisfied himself that the petition was in accordance with its object. The long list of names was written on a separate sheet, and he did not think it necessary to check over all the names.

> As soon as I heard of the facts ... I made inquiry, and desired particulars; the clerk has admitted the whole case, and has expressed his deepest sorrow and regret at having been the instrument in so improper an act, and for having led me into error by not informing me of the alteration he had made in the list.[55]

The whole affair was becoming something of a family feud. The matter was reviewed in *The Law Magazine* and Lord Llanover's stance was attacked in some quarters. It was thought that the dispute had been 'carried on with

---

53 Letter from Lord Llanover to the Lord Chancellor, dated 9th December 1862
54 *The Jurist*
55 Letter from Lord Llanover to the Lord Chancellor from Gt Stanhope St, dated 9th December 1862

all the peculiarities of tone which generally distinguish a family squabble.'

In November and December 1862 Mr Jones, using his assumed name, sent letters to the Lord Chancellor pleading with him to order his surname to be changed in the Commission of the Peace 'at a convenient time'. Referring to the case, an excerpt from *The Times* reads as follows:

> *In Mr. Herbert's case he has done a legal act, and has done all that the law required of him to do,—namely, to act in good faith, with an innocent purpose, and to give reasonably sufficient publicity to his act. By so doing his change of name was legally complete. But he is to be forced to go to the Home Office and pay fees on the republication of the same act, or he and his sons are to be disqualified to hold office in their own county![56]*

In February 1863 the Lord Chancellor ordered the Secretary of Commissions to write to William Herbert. In spite of Lord Llanover's objection, it seems that the alteration of Mr Jones's name on the Commission of Sewers had not been reversed and he was listed 'under the name and description of "William Herbert of Clytha, Esquire."'

> *The Lord Chancellor is therefore of opinion that these circumstances render your case a peculiar and exceptional one, and that as he cannot permit the same gentleman to be called by two different names in two commissions from the Crown, he must alter your name in the Commission of the Peace for the county of Monmouth, and make your description therein the same as your name and description in the commission so recently issued by the order of her Majesty.[57]*

'The wretched farce'[58] was reaching its conclusion by the end of March. Lord Llanover had wanted to raise the matter in the House of Lords, but ...

> *The Martyr of Monmouthshire has established, in defiance of his persecutor the right which Englishmen are commonly supposed to enjoy, of pleasing themselves in all things which are not forbidden by the law of the land ... The House of Lords, though probably sensible of the honour which it derives from the presence of one of its most recent members, is not disposed to concern itself with his little county squabbles.[59]*

Lord Llanover was thought by this time to have ended 'his crusade against the unlicensed assumption of the name Herbert', his 'absurd proceeding'

---

56 Supplement to an *Essay on Surnames, 1863*
57 ibid
58 *The Jurist, September 1863*
59 *The Saturday Review*

being attributed to a natural reaction to the recovery of his personal independence after years of being dictated to by the Marylebone vestry!

The Season drew to a close towards the end of June, and the last drawing-room was held on the afternoon of 23rd June. While reporting this, *The Belfast News-letter* took the opportunity to mock the Llanovers once again.

> ... Lady Llanover's melancholy dancing-parties will be reckoned with the past. Her ladyship has endeavoured this season again to revive the economical entertainments, which she was the first to inaugurate ... namely, afternoon parties, instead of midnight balls.

Friends were to arrive by four o'clock and leave by eight. Dancing was held in the 'stuffy drawing-rooms of Great Stanhope Street' with coffee and ices being served. It was 'a very dull and stupid affair,' wrote the correspondent.

> ... and the afternoon parties are voted ... a decided bore by the votaries of fashion, who would much rather pass the time in Rotten Row or Bond Street, or even at the Botanical Gardens in the Regent's Park.

The Llanover Cymreigyddion held an eisteddfod in October. A tent large enough to hold 500 people was erected on land at Brynhyfryd Farm, on the Llanover estate, with an arch of evergreens over the entrance. On the arch, picked out in different coloured flowers, were the words 'Cymreigyddion Llanover'. The day of the eisteddfod[60] was fine, and the meeting began at eleven o'clock when the President, the vicar of Llanover, took his seat on the platform, with Lady Llanover on his right and the Rev. D. Howell, *Llawdden*,[61] on his left. They were greeted by a rousing rendition of *Rhyfelgyrch Gwyr Harlech* [The March of the Men of Harlech] sung by the Llanover choir to harp accompaniment. The whole front row was taken up by the Llanover and Llanarth families, and members of the clergy. During the morning there were competitions for choirs and harpists, recitations, and extempore speaking. For the latter, the President gave a subject on which the competitor was allowed three to four minutes to speak. The end of the allotted time was marked by the ringing of a bell, 'which caused the greatest diversion'.[62]

After a break to allow for 'rest and recuperation' the tent was once again filled to capacity and the afternoon proceedings began 'with the greatest

---

60   24th October 1863
61   Rev. D. Howell, *Llawdden*, 1831-1903, Vicar of Cardiff
62   *The Cambrian Journal*, 1863

spirit.' The audience was treated to a 'little poetical dialogue in Welsh' by Masters Bleiddian and Arthur Herbert, 'two lovely children of about the ages of six and seven years'.[63] Bleiddian stepped forward first and climbed on a chair in front of the platform. In answer to a question from his grandmother, Lady Llanover, he said, in a clear voice-

> *Cymro wyf a Chymro fyddaf*
> *A Chymraeg yw'r iaith a garaf*
> *A daethum i'm dwy chwaer gael gweled*
> *Fy mod yn caru y wlad y'm ganed*

> A Welshman I am and a Welshman I will be
> And Welsh is the language I love
> And I came to my two sisters to be able to see
> That I love the land of my birth

Then it was Arthur's turn. He took his brother's place on the chair and answered his grandmother thus:

> *Cymru yw fy ngwlad a'm cartre,*
> *Cymru wyf yn Caru oreu.*

> Wales is my country and my home,
> Wales I love the best.

Lady Llanover then gave an address in Welsh, her clear voice reaching to every part of the tent. Her subject was 'the antiquity and excellence of the Cymric language ... one of the most perfect and comprehensive of living languages' the cultivation of which was beneficial, and it was effective for moral purposes! There were eloquent speeches by *Llawdden* and the Rev. D. Charles, vicar of Abercarn, and the meeting was enlivened by the harp and singing competitions.

There were 150 competitors altogether, and all the thirty-five prizes were awarded. Lady Llanover, Mr R. Hall, Lord Llanover's brother (his Lordship being in Scotland at the time), Miss Johnes of Dolaucothi, and the Misses Herbert of Llanarth were amongst those investing each winner with a ribbon and purse. The afternoon meeting ended at six o'clock, but by half past seven the lighted tent was once again full. There were speeches, performances by the various winning harpists and singers, and the evening ended promptly at 10 o'clock

---

63   Bleiddian Herbert, 1858-1931, and Arthur Herbert, 1855-?

...after one of the most delightful days ever remembered in the parish of Llanover, and it is worthy of special notice that not a single instance of even an approach to intoxication was seen or heard during the day.'[64]

For some time there had been a dispute between Lord Llanover and the Rev. John Griffiths, perpetual curate of the parish of Mynyddislwyn. The village of Abercarn was part of the parish, and the Welsh Church there had been built at Lord Llanover's expense. The Church was 'for the express purpose of providing for the religious wants of the Welsh population,'[65] with the services being conducted wholly in the Welsh language. In 1862 the curate received 'a valuable preferment' and so someone had to be found to replace him. A new curate was found, but it seems that before he could take up his duties the permission of the perpetual curate, the Rev. John Griffiths, was needed. He would only give permission if one service would be conducted in English. It goes without saying that Lord Llanover would not agree to this, hence the dispute.

One of his Lordship's chaplains had been taking the services at the Church for a few months, but when it became obvious that the dispute could not be resolved, Lord Llanover decided to transfer the Church to the Calvinistic Methodists, but laid down conditions! The Church of England style of worship must be followed 'as far as is consistent with the Calvinistic Methodist creed.' The first of the new services was held at the end of October 1862, with the Rev. L. Edwards, president of Bala College, and the Rev. Thomas Phillips, of Hereford, officiating. Lord and Lady Llanover were present, of course, together with many of the local clergy and gentry.

Lady Llanover had always been able to reconcile her patriotism and support for Wales with her loyalty to the British crown and she was often involved with presentations to the Royal family. When the Princess of Wales was presented with 'the national token of South Wales', on the 1st March 1864, it was Lady Llanover who, representing the county of Monmouth, carried the casket containing the jewels. There were also ladies representing the counties of Brecon, Cardigan and Radnor amongst the retinue. The Dowager Countess of Dunraven, representing Glamorgan, made the presentation to her Royal Highness who, after examining the jewels with interest, gave them her unqualified approval. The 'token' comprised two beautiful pieces of jewellery; a brooch and a bracelet of emeralds and diamonds, both contained in

---

64 *The Cambrian Journal, 1863*
65 *The Leeds Mercury*

'a very elaborate chased casket', towards which 'every class of her Majesty's loyal and devoted Welsh subjects' had contributed.[66]

England, Scotland and Ireland had erected memorials to the Prince Consort, and early in 1864 George White, the mayor of Tenby, decided that Wales should do the same. It was funded by public subscription and by March 1865 there were over 1000 names on the subscription list including the likes of Lord and Lady Tredegar, Lord Dynevor, Mr Crawshay Bailey and, of course, Lady Llanover. The sculptor was John Evan Thomas of Brecon and George Thomas of Pembroke built it. The mayor laid the first stone on the 14th December 1864, the third anniversary of Prince Albert's death, and in a hole cut in the stone was placed a bottle containing a vellum scroll, on which were inscribed the date, the names of the committee and other details of the project.

Tenby Memorial to Prince Albert
Image reproduced by kind permission
of Kevin Thomas

The base of the memorial consists of three large Welsh marble slabs forming steps, on top of which is the pedestal. According to a report in the *Leeds Mercury* the pedestal was to be made of Welsh marble, with four Sicilian marble panels on the sides. However, another source[67] states that the pedestal is of limestone. The statue itself, standing about nine feet tall, is Sicilian marble.

The memorial was inaugurated on the 2nd August 1865, by Prince Arthur,[68] who represented her Majesty the Queen and it was confidently felt 'that the memorial will be one worthy of the great and good Prince ... and the people of Wales ... '

In September 1866 the *Caledonian Mercury* announced that Lady Llanover

---

66 The *Liverpool Mercury*
67 *Public Monument and Sculpture Association* website
68 Prince Arthur, 1850-1942, he was said to be Queen Victoria's favourite son

was 'coming out' as the authoress of a cookery book, 'in which, no doubt, we shall be told how to compound a Welsh rabbit, and how to make soup out of leeks.' In October *The Times* carried an advertisement for the book, and in January 1867 the following appeared:

> *Good Cookery,*[69] *by the Right Hon. Lady Llanover, is now ready at all booksellers, in large post 8vo,. 500pp with Illustrations, 10s. 6d. Richard Bentley, publisher in ordinary to Her Majesty*

The Pall Mall Gazette stated that the book was 'so put together as to tempt anyone to get through it all at one sitting'; that it was 'pleasantly written'; and that it contained 'a variety of capital recipes ... for all kinds of dishes.' The following month *The Daily News* wrote:

> *The volume contains a great deal of very lively reading: whether the recipes are equally excellent, we must leave it to cooks and housewives to say. There are certainly things in it enough to make one sympathetically hungry ...*

However, as might be expected, *The Belfast News-letter* wrote;

> *That the noble author should have any special information on the subject of her book has evoked the intense astonishment of her friends, as she is known to be the person who introduced morning dancing parties, at which tea, coffee, and ice were the only refreshments provided ...*

Lady Llanover had written this book in response to 'numerous inquiries and applications, from friends, for information about certain simple dishes ... the appearance of which has been hastened by recent urgent demands for a receipt, *How to make a Cook?'* The Author did not claim to write 'a Tale', the book being 'for the avowed purpose of instruction in Cookery, Domestic Economy, and other matters involving home comfort ...' and she made no apology for making public 'practical instructions which are the result of many years' individual experience ...'

It is hardly a cookery book as we think of one today. It is a contrived story of a Traveller, in Wales for the first time, meeting the Hermit of the Cell of St Gover. Having benefited from the Hermit's hospitality, the Traveller wished to be taught the methods used by the Hermit to produce the tasty, nourishing meals he experienced while there. Utensils such as the digester, the double saucepan, and the *ffwrn fach* [lit. small oven] are illustrated[70] and their use

---

69 *The First Principles of Good Cookery,* Lady Llanover
70 These illustrations are signed E.J. Possibly Elizabeth (Betha) Johnes

described. In the Author's own words, the narrative passes on 'to the relation of the Hermit's dinners - what they were, and how they were cooked'. Nothing was wasted, and every last ounce of goodness was extracted from the wholesome ingredients. All the while, the Traveller was taking notes, and these appear in the second section of the book. Finally, the Appendix contains the recipes: Roast Leg of Mutton, and Root of Tongue Soup; Bread Sauce, and Boiled Eggs; the Welsh Hermit's Favourite Chicken and Leek Pie; all as prepared and cooked in the Hermit's [Lady Llanover's?] kitchen.

The whole book seems to have been an excuse for Lady Llanover to express her firmly held beliefs, her strong opinions, and her sometimes eccentric ideas. Besides all the excellent advice about economy and healthy eating she expressed an opinion on a variety of subjects ranging from the bad practice of removing hedges from the roadsides, to bemoaning the fact that no good shirtmakers could be found; from the danger of travelling by train, to the art of bee-keeping. The book contains a good deal of common sense and practicality, as useful in the 21st century as it was in the days of Lady Llanover herself.

In her introduction she says, ' had time and circumstances permitted, this book would have been more complete, but, ... the Author decided on publishing one volume as quickly as possible, without waiting to rearrange the subjects or to improve the composition ...' The reason for her haste was to become obvious.

When she and her husband went to London, in November 1866, his Lordship was in his usual state of good health. As a keen sportsman he had suffered several accidents, on one occasion being thrown from his horse, on another losing an eye. However, he had a strong constitution and recovered well from these incidents. His most recent accident happened when he was shooting. He was using a new gun, which 'kicked' and hit his cheek. This happened twice in a short space of time, hitting his face in the same place each time. A tumour appeared in his cheek, apparently as a result of the blows from the gun, and just after Christmas 1866 he was advised to have an operation to remove it. Although it was a very painful procedure he faced it 'with wonderful fortitude'[71] but unfortunately the operation was not a complete success and some of the tumour remained. Betha Johnes wrote in her diary:

On Saturday, Sir William Fergusson [1808-1877] burnt out the abscess in

---

71   *The Cambrian*

poor Lord Llanover's face with caustic after aqua fortis [nitric acid], fearing to use the knife on account of the loss of blood. He suffered agonies ...[72]

His general health being so good, his Lordship's doctors had no qualms about advising another operation to remove what was left of the tumour and on the 21st January 1867 he underwent another painful procedure. In spite of his good health, and much to the dismay of his doctors, the wound would not heal. Over the next few months the extreme pain and difficulty in eating 'enfeebled his robust constitution'. He longed to return to his beloved Llanover but was much too ill to be moved, and at 3.30am on the 27th April 1867 this genial gentleman, 'the friend, benefactor, and supporter of all those about him,' was released from his suffering. 'All is over,' said Lady Llanover, 'the light of my life is gone.'[73]

Lord Llanover's death at 9 Great Stanhope Street was due to epithelioma of the cheek, and was certified by J. Jones, MD, who had been present at the death. It is interesting to note that Dr Jones's address was the Homeopathic Hospital, Great Ormond Street.

The Llanovers' large circle of friends had repeatedly enquired after him during his illness; even the Queen of the Netherlands asked to be kept informed, and on receiving the sad news, sent a telegram to Lady Llanover saying:

Deep regrets for the ever lamented friend. May God comfort you.[74]

Queen Victoria and the Prince of Wales were amongst those who expressed their concern, and after his Lordship's death Lady Llanover received an 'autograph letter' from the Queen 'expressive of her deep sympathy, and of her Majesty's appreciation of Lord Llanover when a minister of the Crown.'[75]

---

72 *THSC Session 1964, Part I,* 'Lord Llanover (Big Ben) in London', Maxwell Fraser

73 *Arglwyddes Llanofer,* Rachel Ley. From Lord Llanover's Last Years, Maxwell Fraser

74 *The Cambrian*

75 *The Liverpool Mercury*

Chapter 5
Lady Llanover, Widow
(1867-1896)

Poor Lady Llanover has gone through much, and it was like her usual unselfishness to keep sorrow from us all.[1]

Doubtless, when the Treorky [sic] Choir leader astonished the Queen [Victoria] by being obliged to admit his choir could not sing the Welsh version of ... the National Anthem, it was thinking of the effect such a damaging admission would have made on the mind of her venerable friend Lady Llanofer, that caused her Majesty to laugh so hearty.[2]

Lord Llanover had left instructions that his funeral was to be 'perfectly private in the strictest sense of the word.' These were written in November 1861 when he was in excellent health and had no reason to think they would be implemented for many years.

My funeral to be as plain and inexpensive as possible; my body is to be carried by such of my tenants and labourers as may be selected for the purpose, and who may desire to bear it; the pall-bearers to be agents, tenants; no hat bands or scarves to be used by anybody; no hired carriages; no hired people; no parade of Volunteers; Welsh hymns to be sung at intervals, from the time the body is carried out of the house until it is deposited in its last resting place ... Our good Queen gave to her subjects an example which they will do well to follow, when her aunt, the Duchess of Gloucester, and her excellent mother, the Duchess of Kent, died. The funerals of those illustrious personages were conducted as privately as possible. Why should we, her subjects, contemplate funereal splendour?[3]

During the following months Lady Llanover received many messages of condolence. The Queen herself ...

... addressed an autograph letter to Lady Llanover, expressive of her deep sympathy, and of her Majesty's appreciation of the services of Lord Llanover when a minister of the Crown.[4]

---

1   *THSC, 'Lord Llanover (Big Ben) in London', Maxwell Fraser*
2   *The Western Mail*
3   *The Cambrian*
4   *The Liverpool Mercury*

There was also a message from the incumbent and congregation of the Welsh Church in London to which Her Ladyship replied in Welsh. A translation of her letter appeared in *The Cambrian* on the 12th June 1867, from which the following excerpt is taken:

The sentiments expressed towards my beloved husband are valued by me not only as a memorial of the sympathy felt for myself by our Welsh countrymen in whose welfare he ever evinced such a special interest, but as a valuable record of their expressed opinion of his services with reference to the Welsh Church, to which, for so many years he proved his regard.

Not long after the sad event, Lady Llanover presented Welsh bibles to all her tenants in memory of her beloved Benjamin, and the words that were engraved on his coffin were printed on a plate inside the cover. The bibles were printed by Oxford University Press for the British and Foreign Bible Society and were available, to subscribers only, from their warehouse in Blackfriars, London.

Lord Llanover's will was proved in the Probate Court of London by her Ladyship, John Johnes of Dolaucothi and Mr Henry Ray Freshfield, of Bank Buildings, London.

The will is dated December 28, 1866, and, in the fewest words, leaves all his lordship's property, real and personal, 'to his most dear and devotedly-attached wife, Baroness Llanover.'[5]

Is it possible that his Lordship amended his will when he realised how serious his condition was?

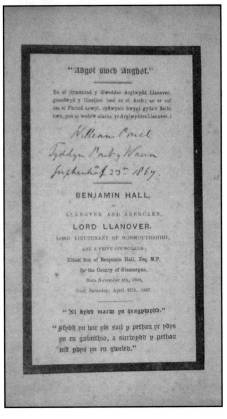

*Inside cover of a bible
in memory of Lord Llanover*

Henry Brinley Richards was born in Carmarthen in 1817. He showed much musical promise and at the 1834 Cardiff Eisteddfod he won a prize for his variations on the old Welsh tune *Llwyn Onn* [The Ash Grove]. Under the

5   *The Daily News*

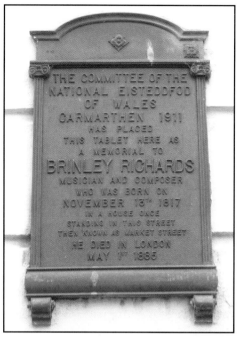

*House on the site where
Brinley Richards was born.*

*Memorial to Brinley Richards placed on the
house on the site where he was born.*

Photographs: Iain MacFarlaine

patronage of the Duke of Newcastle, he studied at the Royal Academy in London, then went to Paris to study, where he became a pupil of Chopin. On his return to London he became an instructor at the Royal Academy and later a director. Unlike some who achieved fame beyond Wales, Brinley Richards did not forget his roots. Among his many compositions the most well known today must be *God Bless the Prince of Wales,* composed in 1862 and advertised in *The Penny Illustrated* under the heading 'New Music' in January 1863. Although largely forgotten after the abdication crisis in 1936, it was recalled in a spontaneous rendition by the spectators at the 1958 Empire Games in Cardiff when the Queen announced that Prince Charles was to become the Prince of Wales.

Brinley Richards' collection *Songs of Wales (Caneuon Cymru)* was first published in 1867, his intention being 'to supplement and not to supersede previous collections'. Sir Walter Scott was among the many eminent writers of the English words and John *Ceiriog* Hughes[6] wrote the Welsh.

---

6   John *Ceiriog* Hughes, 1832-1887

The new symphonies and arrangements by Mr. Richards, it is needless to say, are in perfect harmony with the spirit of the old melodies, and it is to be regretted that the work should suffer from grave typographical errors ... even in the title page, 'Caneuon Cymru' being transformed into 'Canenon Cymru' ... On the whole, Mr. Richards' work must be pronounced of the highest value to students of Cambrian minstrelsie, and it cannot fail to add fresh lustre to the musical reputation of the Welsh people.[7]

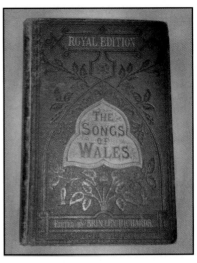

Another edition was published in 1873, and a *Royal Edition* in 1879.

The Songs of Wales, Royal Edition

Brinley Richards was asked to engage certain London artistes to appear at the Carmarthen Eisteddfod of 1867, which took place from the 3rd to the 6th September. He submitted a list of names to the Eisteddfod committee who then decided whom to invite. Naturally, these artistes decided for themselves which pieces to perform, and their choices did not please Mr Edward Joseph, one of the National Eisteddfod secretaries. He took it upon himself to write to *The London Standard* with a thinly-veiled criticism of Mr Richards, accusing him of 'a lack of patriotism, in having given but a very small place to Welsh music in the programmes of the evening concerts.' *The Cambrian* hurried to the defence of Mr Richards, and the following is an excerpt from the article it published:

A vocalist will know what he or she can sing with best effect; and if Mr. Joseph imagines that artistes of such position ... were likely to sing exclusively Welsh Music, he is affected with a degree of credulity which entitles him to the commiseration of the public and the anxious attention of his friends. Mr. Richards himself played Welsh Music; but like a true artiste he did not confine himself to that. He was desirous that his countrymen should have an opportunity of becoming acquainted with the masterpieces of such composers as Weber and Mendelssohn.

The article went on to say that it would have been utterly impossible to repay Mr Richards for all the work he had done for the Eisteddfod. He had received an honorarium, but that would in no way cover his expenses,

---

7   *North Wales Chronicle*

incurred in travelling and attending rehearsal. It concluded:

> *If the highest talent which the musical world can afford was to be presented to a Welsh audience, what could Mr Richards do? Was he to pay German artistes to study Welsh music expressly for the Eisteddfod. The narrow-minded clique who have been silly enough to bring unjust accusations against a talented, but generous patriot, would soon (were they to have their way) expose Eisteddfodau to all the ridicule which their enemies at present endeavour unfairly to cast upon them.*

A correspondent from *The Musical World* was at the Eisteddfod and his first article appeared in the edition of the 7th September. He described the setting in a field adjoining Priory Road.

> *... there stands a huge wooden building, circular in shape, and capable of holding some 6,000 persons ... such an edifice, or, indeed, any edifice at all, is a concession to the weakness of modern times and men. At the Eisteddfodau of old the peaceful contests were carried on in the open air with a supreme contempt for weather which, in those days, was only equalled by a supreme in-difference to dirt.*

Inside the Pavilion, when all were seated, a trumpeter tried to perform a fanfare 'and signally failed.' This was followed by the National Anthem 'most hideously played by a brass band.' After a short speech, in English, by the President, Mr D. Pugh, MP, *Llew Llwyfo* made an appearance and sang a Welsh song, known in English as *Cambria's Holiday,* – very badly! However, the writer was impressed with the way in which everyone joined in the chorus.

> *The effect of the multitude of voices, keeping excellent time, and singing very generally in parts, was absolutely impressive, and formed, to me at least, one of the striking features of the proceedings.*

As the piece was intended for *The Musical World* the writer naturally concentrated on the musical items and was fair in his praise and his criticism. The fourteen-year-old who won the competition for female pianists, Miss Lizzie Moulding, of Castle Bailey Street, Swansea, played 'with a feeling and expression which proved her to be a real artist.' However, one of the choral competitions proved to be something of a farce! The competitors could not be 'rounded up', much to the annoyance of the 'masters of the ceremonies.' Eventually one of the choirs was found, the others having been held up somewhere on the railway, and that lone choir performed well enough to be awarded the prize. Later there should have been a competition for the triple harp, but, sadly, only one North Walian harper put in an appearance. 'Only one triple harpist at a National Eisteddfod! Alack the day!!' commented the writer.

Lady Llanover was invited to attend the Celtic International Congress in St Brieuc, Brittany, in October 1867, but quite understandably she did not accept. The organisers had asked that she send *Gruffydd*, her harper, which she did, and also his fifteen-year-old daughter, Susanna, and their performances at the Congress were greeted with 'the most lively applause.' The President thanked 'the respected lady for her obliging compliance' and his call for 'a triple round of applause … excited the warmest enthusiasm among the auditory. The three cheers were given with a heartiness of unanimity which showed that one heart beat in all their breasts.'[8]

It was Lady Llanover's custom to give tea and cakes to the day school and Sunday school pupils at Abercarn on St David's Day. In spite of all she had suffered in the previous year she continued the custom in 1868. Over 500 persons, each carrying a leek, were served with an abundance of tea and excellent cake in the beautifully-decorated school. Later, there was a very interesting meeting where there was singing and recitation. *Gruffydd* was there to play the harp, having been sent over from Llanover by her Ladyship especially for the occasion.[9] Ten years later her Ladyship spent a week in Abercarn visiting 'the schools and other institutions connected with that part of her estate.' While there she paid particular attention to the new coffee tavern, *Cloch Gobaith*, the former Bell Inn, where there were now no intoxicating drinks to be found! It was established to 'promote habits of temperance … and [was] fitted with cooking apparatus and all appliances necessary to provide tea, coffee, soup, and the cooking of meat.' On the signboard was the following verse:

Dyma le i bawb gael te,
Bara chaws a menyn,
Aelwyd lân yn llawn o dân
A mêl oddiwrth y gwenyn. [10]

[Here is a place for everyone to have tea, bread, cheese and butter,
A clean hearth full of fire and honey from the bees.][11]

Lady Llanover's interest in politics continued after her husband's death.

---

8 *The Cambrian*

9 *Baner ac Amserau Cymru*

10 *Pontypridd District Herald.* My thanks to Dean Powell for these snippets

11 A rough translation by the author

In the General Election of 1868[12] Colonel Clifford was the Liberal candidate for Monmouthshire.

A report was circulated that some of the agents of the Pontypool estates were canvassing for the Tories, that the widowed Mrs Hanbury Leigh supported the Tories, and that her son had been brought up in Tory principles. On hearing this, Mrs Leigh wrote to Lady Llanover as follows:

> *I feel sure that the report about our agents working for the Tories must be an invention of some ill-natured person. They all know that we are thoroughgoing Liberals, and the tenants themselves are advanced liberals, so I think there can be no doubt the report is false ... everybody belonging to us [is] allowed to vote according to his own way of thinking. I believe the Pontypool people are nearly all on the Liberal side. In former years Mr. Leigh always said the same, viz., that he wished everybody to vote as he pleased, and that is what we wish now.*[13]

Mrs Leigh regretted that her son was not yet old enough to follow in his father's footsteps as representative for the county. Lady Llanover was said to be 'heart and soul in the cause' and she was 'with them hand and glove; and ... the houses of Clytha and Llanarth were with them to the backbone.'

New Year's Eve 1868 was celebrated in Abercarn with a literary meeting of a wholly Welsh character, with the support of Lady Llanover. It was the first such meeting to be held there and was more successful than the committee could have hoped, the room proving too small for such a crowd. The refinement and elegance of the musical compositions made up for the childish, but promising, aspect of the compositions on other subjects.

The chairman, the Rev. D. Saunders, was very critical of the 'wrongly named' Welsh National Eisteddfod for spending the Principality's money on anything but the Welsh and their language and for bringing strangers to sing pieces they could not understand. What, he wondered, would the English think if they were offered a similar insult! A *Welsh* eisteddfod should nurture the native talent and present it to the world in its own proper style. [It seems he was on the side of those critical of Brinley Richards!]

Gruffydd, Lady Llanover's harper, played several Welsh airs, in his own masterly fashion. Everyone was grateful to her Ladyship for sending him to entertain them, and also for giving most of the prizes. She also promised prizes for the next meeting, planned for the summer.[14]

---

12 Polling took place between 17th November and 7th December 1868

13 *The Daily News*

14 *Baner ac Amserau Cymru*

Almost two years after the tragic and unexpected death of Lord Llanover her Ladyship suffered another bereavement. She had already lost her husband and her two sons, one only five years old, and now her grandson, Stephan Sulien Herbert, died from pulmonary and abdominal tuberculosis.[15] He was just four years old and his short life is remembered by an inscription on the seat near the Llanover tomb, which is dedicated to his mother's memory.[16]

In *Carnhuanawc's* 'musical reminiscences' he wrote of the harp and of how the coming of Methodism had changed people's habits. In his aunt's day, in the middle of the 18th century young people enjoyed dancing to harp and fiddle accompaniment. He remembered two harpers, each playing the triple harp, Thomas Blayney,[17] harper to the Earl of Powys, and a man by the name of Ricketts.[18] The Methodists frowned upon the dancing and jollity, and caused some dissenters to turn away from harp playing.

> *My father told me that he remembered an old man ... who played the harp,[19] but who joined the Methodists or Dissenters and then gave up the harp, and threw it under the bed, where it lay till it got unglued and worm-eaten and fell to pieces.*

By 1869 the triple harp was 'fast falling into desuetude.' Brinley Richards had been asked to secure the services of a Welsh triple harper to play at a Welsh banquet in London and he was dismayed and mortified to discover that there was not one real Welsh harp, nor a real Welsh harper to be found in the whole of London. As a result he wrote to the newspapers 'complaining of the discouragement given to the triple-stringed harp by a body calling themselves "The Council of the National Eisteddfod"'. As a result of 'agitation … to do something for this national instrument' some influential Welsh families, Welsh journals and even the Eisteddfod Council were 'taking up the matter warmly.' One result of this was the appointment of *Gruffydd*, Lady Llanover's family harper, as 'Welsh Harper Extraordinary' to the Prince of Wales. He was said to be 'one of the few still living who have never deserted the fine national instrument of the principality' and who continued to play

---

15 Stephan Sulien Carolus Herbert died at Llanover 6th April 1869
16 The Hon. Augusta Herbert, 1824-1912
17 Thomas Blayney, Montgomeryshire, won 30 guineas at the Carmarthen Eisteddfod in 1819.
     He is said to have introduced the triple harp to South Wales when he moved there
18 Possibly John Ricketts from Llanidloes
19 It is not noted whether or not this was a triple harp

in the 'true style of playing ... handed down from time immemorial ... in succession from master to pupil.' *Gruffydd's* harp was a faithful copy of the harps made by John Richard(s)[20] of Llanrwst ...

> ... *one of which, still preserved, was played upon and belonged to the celebrated harper Blind Parry, of Rhivaton [sic], whose exquisite playing is recorded by the poet Gray, who said that it had given the finishing stimulus to his poem 'The Bard' in 1755.*[21]

Also, a circular was issued by 'the new and energetic secretary to the Eisteddfod,' Mr Mostyn Williams, which drew attention to a letter from Brinley Richards, and an article that appeared in *The Carnarfon and Denbigh Herald* that said:

> *The object of preserving our national instrument, and restoring, if possible, its ancient prestige, must commend itself to the favourable consideration of every true patriot.*[22]

The nation's debt to Lady Llanover, for her support and promotion of Welsh music and literature, was acknowledged, as was the fact that she and Sir H. Williams[23] of Bodelwyddan Hall retained the ancient custom of employing a domestic harper, and that in other private families 'the playing of our national instrument is cultivated as an accomplishment.' In the circular, Mr Williams deplored the fact that those few examples of the old instrument still to be found were considered to be 'objects of curiosity and relics of bygone days, [rather] than instruments to be played upon in this mechanical and utilitarian age.' It was announced that in future the Welsh harp was to be an important feature in the eisteddfodau. Also, Brinley Richards was to be responsible for music at the 1870 Brecon Eisteddfod where there was to be a competition for the best triple harp 'which shall combine elegance of design, beauty of adornment, sweetness of tone, and economy.' The Eisteddfod council would also 'endeavour to establish a department for the qualification of teachers, and do all in their power to restore the harp to its ancient position.' Everyone interested in the subject was invited to co-operate and send in any practical suggestions.

This was a 'call to arms' for Lady Llanover and although at the time she was 'prostrated by domestic affliction' and struggling 'against an unchanging

---

20 John Richard(s), 1711-1789, Llanrwst

21 *The Liverpool Mercury*

22 *The Cambrian*

23 Sir H. Williams, 1802-1876, brother of Mrs Lucy of Charlecote.

sorrow', she lost no time in starting her campaign to save the old harp, a campaign that continued to the end of her days. In June 1869 *The Liverpool Mercury* published the following:

> *Lady Llanover has offered a prize of a triple-stringed Welsh harp for the best player on the instrument. No one will be allowed to compete who has ever played upon the pedal harp. It is announced that the competition is distinct from any public meeting or 'English Eisteddfods' or 'councils or committees of management connected with such meetings.'*

Invitations were sent to the 'real Welsh harpers to assemble with their triple-stringed harps to compete for the prize of a new Welsh triple-stringed harp, to be given by her ladyship.'

> *All were to play the unrivalled Welsh air of 'Difyrwch Gwyr Harlech' (The March of the Men of Harlech) without variations, as no printed variations exist in the Welsh style; the only variations published being modern Anglicised arrangements, which entirely alter the character of the original music. No one being allowed to compete who had ever played on the pedal harp.*[24]

There was also to be free *Ymborth a Lletty* [board and lodgings] for three days for all competitors.

'Lady Llanover's Eisteddfod'[25] took place on Thursday, 14th October 1869, in the magnificent hall of Llanover House. At one end of the hall, on a low platform, stood the prize harp, adorned with a garland of flowers. *Gruffydd*, one of the judges, sat on another platform in the bay window, wearing 'full costume, covered with medals won in days of yore'. The body of the hall was filled by the estate tenants, while to left and right Lady Llanover's guests were seated – her family and house guests, and the Llanarth family. The tinkling of a silver bell announced the entry of Her Ladyship and she took her seat to the strains of a martial Welsh air played by the harp chorus. The company having settled down, the 'Welsh choir in the gallery burst forth with the spirit-stirring strains of *Codiad yr Haul* [The Rising of the Sun].' Lady Llanover then addressed those present in Welsh, her clear voice reaching each corner of the hall. She explained her reason for her invitation to the 'true and real harpers of Wales', which was 'to give support and encouragement to the most perfect national instrument in the world.' It was Mr Brinley Richards, she said, who felt it his duty 'to call the attention of the entire Principality, through

---

24 *The Cambrian*
25 *The Western Mail*

the newspapers, to the actual danger of losing altogether this national instrument, unrivalled and precious.' Her Ladyship stated her belief that the national instrument of a country should be light enough for the player to carry.

The triple harp of Wales possesses this excellence, and there is no other national instrument to compare with it which combines the same power with such sweet harmony, and yet is so light as to enable the player to carry it for miles on foot. It is necessary to have an ass and a cart, or a car (or at least a wheelbarrow), to bring a pedal harp from one street to another, it is so loaded with steel and brass; but the triple-stringed harp of our country can be carried on the shoulders up our mountains and down our valleys.[26]

But the *false* eisteddfodau, said her Ladyship, would not have been able to do so much harm to the triple harp if the Welsh harpers themselves had stood firm and decided never to abandon their national instrument!

The competition then began, each harper playing individually the *March of the Men of Harlech*. Eight harpers had come to the meeting, some from North Wales and some from the South, and although he did not compete, Richard Pugh,[27] harper to Sir Hugh Williams, Bart., of Bodelwyddan, was there, and 'sat like a patriarch at the head of the competitors.' Two of the harpers were disqualified right away as they played the pedal harp. The judges, Brinley Richards and *Gruffydd,* could not decide between three of the harpers, and those three were asked to play again. Abraham Rees, from Merthyr Tydfil, who was fourteen years old that day, had been taught by his father, and he was declared the winner. Robert Jones of Bala was second, and Lewis Williams of Pontllanfraith third. There were just three prizes offered, but Lady Llanover's generosity would not allow any of the competitors to go away empty handed. E. Pugh was given the handsome sum of five pounds and ...

... her Ladyship was pleased to offer John Roberts – who was not pleased with the decision of the judges – £3, and £1 to his son, but he would not accept it, nor allow his son to accept his portion.[28]

John Roberts thought he should have been allowed to play again, as his harp was set in the wrong key!

Abraham Rees's prize was the beautiful triple harp made by Elias Francis, son of John Francis, himself a harp maker of note, having been taught by

---

26 *The Cambrian*
27 Richard Pugh, brother of Hugh Pugh who was successful at the Cardiff Eisteddfod in 1834
28 *The Western Mail*

Carnhuanawc. He also received a gift of two pounds, given by Miss Jane Williams, Aberpergwm. Five pounds, given by Sir Hugh Williams, Bodelwyddan, was presented to Robert Jones and four pounds, given by John Johnes, Dolaucothi, to Lewis Williams. John Roberts, senior, received a set of harp strings, the gift of R. C. Hall[29] and £1, and his young son, a beginner, also received £1. The 'venerable Richard Pugh' then received a largesse from Lady Llanover, who also promised Robert Jones and Lewis Williams a triple harp each.

The prize harp was made in the same shape and manner as the harp made by John Richard(s) of Llanrwst, which was then in Lady Llanover's possession. The wood used had been drying for twenty years, and the harp's antique shape was very strong. Lady Llanover told the assembled people that she believed that they all had a true and sincere desire for the restoration of the triple harp to its rightful place. She was sure, she said, that her own farmers and tenants took an interest, and she would be proud to see a Welsh harp in every house.

Among the distinguished guests were the Rev. D. Howell, vicar of Cardiff, Dr Carl Meyer, John Johnes, Dolaucothi, Mr Rees of Tonn, Brinley Richards and Herr Sjöden,[30] all of whom spoke in favour of supporting the Welsh triple-stringed harp. Ivor Herbert was also there and played his part by calling, in Welsh,

The Gwesty Dirwestol (formerly The Duke)
Photograph: Mrs June Over

for the bards to come forward with *Englynion*,[31] which they did, 'and Welsh verse was poured forth in rapid succession.'[32] That evening the large room of the *Gwesty Dirwestol* [Temperance Hotel][33] was filled to overflowing for a meeting, chaired by Mr Rees of Tonn, where the audience was treated to a

---

29 Richard Crawshay Hall 1804-1884, Lord Llanover's brother
30 Adolf Sjöden, 1843-1893, Swedish harp virtuoso
31 *Englynion* -alliterative stanzas
32 *The Liverpool Mercury*
33 Formerly a Public House

performance by Abraham Rees on his prize harp. There were speeches and singing and the evening ended with the choir singing Brinley Richards' *God Bless the Prince of Wales*.

The Musical Times reported that their sympathies were 'certainly with those who are so energetically devoting both time and money in aid of this thoroughly national movement' and published a letter from Brinley Richards, which began:

> *The favourable manner in which many of the English papers have noticed my appeal for the preservation of an old national instrument – the 'Welsh Triple Harp' – sufficiently indicates that the interest in the subject is not limited to the Principality.[34]*

There was much correspondence in the press from others interested in the harp. Chatterton[35] for instance wrote to *Baner ac Amserau Cymru* in November 1869 commenting on Lady Llanover's Harp Competition. Although he admired 'patriots standing up for everything connected with their country' and sympathised with 'those enthusiasts who do their utmost to uphold an instrument merely because it is their national instrument', he thought such people were not competent to compare it with the same kind of instrument that was more modern. He seemed shocked that a musician such as Brinley Richards, having attended the Royal Academy of Music, and having proved himself to be a 'refined musician' should advocate 'the superior claims of the Welsh triple-stringed harp over that *[sic]* of the pedal harp.' As the triple harp has almost 100 strings, each string is necessarily small, and therefore produces a thin and wiry tone. Also, it is impossible to modulate[36] on a triple harp, except for the occasional use of an accidental.[37] This limitation of the triple harp no doubt accounted for 'the diatonic[38] nature of Welsh national music' and influenced Welsh composers for whatever instrument they were composing. He then wrote of :

> *an amusing incident [that arose] at an orchestral rehearsal in the time of Tom Cooke,[39] when a composition by the late John Parry was being rehearsed. The band had proceeded through the greater portion of the work, when Tom Cooke*

---

34 *The Musical Times*

35 John Balsir Chatterton, 1804-1871

36 Modulate - change from one key to another in the course of a composition

37 Accidental - sign by which a note is chromatically altered by being raised or lowered

38 Diatonic - using only the notes of the prescribed major or minor scale

39 Thomas Cooke, 1782-1848

*exclaimed:- Look out, gentlemen, there is an **accidental** coming!*

He added that he did not relate this with any intention of disparaging the music of Wales, but to illustrate the limitations of the triple harp, which 'naturally crippled the composers.' He thought that the patriotic enthusiasts were wrong to criticise the 'so-called "false Eisteddfod"' for having done nothing to help the survival of the triple harp. To his knowledge prizes of a triple harp and money had been offered at several eisteddfodau that he had attended. At the Swansea Eisteddfod in 1863 his friend and former pupil, John Thomas, undertook the task of securing money to establish a triple harp scholarship; it was to be for ten- to eighteen-year-olds and consisted of a triple harp and 30 guineas towards the musical education of the scholar for one year. John Thomas himself guaranteed the scholarship and among the subscribers were the Dowager Countess of Dunraven, Lady Llanover, Maria Jane Williams and Mrs Lucy of Charlecote. Chatterton pointed out that if John Thomas had not given up the triple harp to concentrate on the pedal harp, he would never have gained such a reputation as a harpist and composer. He had given his country a collection of Welsh melodies, arranged in such a way that they could be performed across Europe. Without his London concerts of Welsh music the world would not have heard the voice of Edith Wynne.[40] Nor would Chatterton himself have shared success with John Thomas, through public performances of his Welsh melodies.

Lady Llanover became really angry with John Thomas because he preferred the pedal harp. He very much regretted the break between them, which had arisen mainly from his 'inability to view matters connected with [his] artistic pursuits in the same light as herself',[41] and never forgot the kindness she showed him at the start of his career.

News of this Grand Harp Competition soon reached Pottsville, Pennsylvania, where Franklin Harris had established a woollen factory. His family, originally from Caerphilly, had moved to Llanover about 1818 where they established a woollen 'manufactory' at Gwenffrwd. It was built on land at Brynhyfryd Farm at the expense of Ann Harris. Franklin went to America about 1843 and by Christmas Eve that year he had 'turned the Beam and put the worp [sic] in the Loom' helped by Edwin Harris, another member of the family. When he read about the harp competition in a newspaper sent to him from Wales he recognised the harp maker's name - Elias Francis.

---

40 Sarah Edith Wynne, *Eos Cymru*, 1842-1897
41 *Lady Llanofer, Gwenynen Gwent,* Rachel Ley. Letter from John Thomas to Betha Johnes in 1896

I [saw] that the harp was built by one I was well acquainted with, when he was a child ... going to Saron Chapel, Goytre, on Sunday mornings, his Father and the boy would mostly go hand in hand, his name is Elias, and he is the son of John Francis ... [42]

Franklin had kept some of the first yard of flannel he produced in America and when he wrote to his nephew, Col Harry H. Davis,[43] he enclosed two samples[44] of that piece of 'all wool Welsh Flannel', one of which he asked to be sent to Lady Llanover, together with its history.

... let me know how is Mother's good friend Lady Llanover, her Ladyship was allways [sic] so good and kind to my Dear Mother, and I shall never forget my Mother's true friends ...

At the beginning of 1870 there was a rumour that Brinley Richards was to be given a knighthood, but he declined the honour. His discovery, in 1870, of an unpublished manuscript by Handel in the British Museum must have caused great excitement among those who supported the triple harp. Handel admired the skill of Powell, Welsh harper to King George II and had 'introduced harp passages into several of his Oratorios.'[45] This newly found work was a concerto for triple harp, written for Powell, and it consisted of 'an allegro, a larghetto, and a Rondo finale.'[46] Lady Llanover soon organised 'a genuine Welsh musical entertainment' held on 15th July 1870 at her London home in Great Stanhope Street. Accompanied by her daughter and grandchildren her Ladyship greeted her distinguished guests who included royalty, foreign ambassadors and the foremost gentry. Lady Llanover's purpose was, of course, to demonstrate the capabilities of the triple harp, and what better way could there be than to present to them a previously unpublished work composed for the instrument by the great Mr Handel; and who better to perform it than the renowned Swedish harper, Herr Sjöden, who performed the whole piece from memory! The *tutti* were two violins, a cello, and a double bass. The entertainment included four songs from Maria Jane Williams' collection of ancient Welsh airs of Gwent and Morganwg. Miss Williams, although an amateur, was an accomplished musician and accompanied the singers at the piano, while Herr Sjöden joined them, playing the triple harp.

---

42 NLW Handlist of Manuscripts. 10982F
43 Col Harry H. Davis, US Consul in Cardiff
44 One piece is now in the NLW
45 *The Musical World*
46 *Dwight's Journal of Music*

In December 1870 *The Graphic* gave its opinion of the concerto. It was unquestionably interesting, they wrote, as an unknown piece by Handel, but they doubted whether Brinley Richards had done the great composer any favours 'in his capacity of resuscitator and editor.'

Scarcely a single new phrase occurs from beginning to end of the work; but instead thereof we have the most hackneyed progressions and sequences characteristic of the time when they were written. The 'orchestral accompaniments' are for a trio of strings, and, as the harp can be played on the piano, Powell's concerto may yet take its place among chamber music.

The writer went on to remark that the concerto, in its original form, and not Brinley Richards' edition of it, had been dedicated to Lady Llanover.

... there is a great deal too much made in a note of the illustrious and noble personages before whom the work was performed in July last. Handel, who was greater than all those illustrious and noble personages put together, needs no patronage ever for his Welsh harp concerto.[47]

At this time there was a movement afoot 'for raising a well-deserved monument to a celebrated Welsh worthy – the Rev. Rees Prichard'[48] and it was decided to hold a grand Eisteddfod in Llandovery in May 1872 in aid of this movement. A large pavilion, able to hold 3,500 people, was erected and although the prizes were not great, 'some of them were sufficiently large to attract powerful choirs and famous singers from a considerable distance.' Mr W. Rees, of Tonn, was vice-president and Brinley Richards, the 'laureate composer of Wales' was the music judge, and he 'performed his arduous duties with his usual grace.'

Today's *eisteddfodwyr* [eisteddfod goers] will be familiar with the sort of weather experienced that day in Llandovery:

Early in the morning the whole land was covered by a dense mist, which developed as the day advanced into a drenching drizzle, which continued off and on till late in the evening.

The reporter noted that in Epsom, Surrey, where the Derby was being run, 'the weather was everything that could be desired!' There was great enthusiasm in Llandovery, however, and the huge pavilion, although sadly not proof against the weather, was crowded. The programme was a very long one and

---

47 *The Graphic*
48 Rhys Prichard, *Yr Hen Ficer*, c 1580-1644. Author of *Canwyll y Cymry*

included competitions for choirs of various ages and numbers, poetry and prose, solo singers and instrumentalists. Lady Llanover, as usual, had shown her support by contributing a prize …

> *For the best translation into Welsh (by former or present pupils of the Welsh Collegiate Institution, Llandovery) of 'Julius Caesar; Act III; Scene II' from Shakespeare. (The metre to be in 'Blank Verse,' the same as the original.)*[49]

The prize of £6 was awarded to *Geraint,* who did not make himself known. The second prize of £2 was won by the Rev. J. M. Prydderch, of Llanarthney, and a third prize of £1, donated by Miss Johnes of Dolaucothi, was awarded to Mr T. D. Lewis, of Dryslwydd.

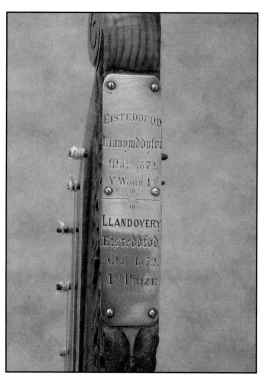

There was, of course, a triple harp competition, the first prize being a triple harp, value £10. 10s. given by Mr and Mrs W. Rees, of Tonn. Mr Richards had already spoken of the ancient national instrument, regretting that it 'had been sadly neglected of late', and praised the 'patriotic devotion' of Lady Llanover in endeavouring to preserve the national instrument of Wales. At this Eisteddfod she gave a prize of five guineas, which was to be awarded to the second best player. There was also a prize of two guineas for the third best and one pound, given by the Marquis of Bute, for each of the unsuccessful harpers in the competition. The competition created a lot of interest and *Y Fronfraith Fach*[50] was awarded the first prize. She was

The harp won by Susanna Gruffydd Richards, Llandovery Eisteddfod 1872

Thanks to Keith Floyd. Photograph: Chris Barlow

Susanna, the eighteen-year-old daughter of the renowned Thomas Griffiths, *Gruffydd,* harper extraordinary to the Prince of Wales, and Lady Llanover's family harper. The concert in the evening was very well attended and among

---

49 *The Cambrian*

50 The little song thrush

the principal performers was *Gruffydd*, the harper from Llanover. Although the music was very good, the audience's enjoyment must have been a little dampened by the ever-falling rain.

In the preface to the Royal Edition of his *Songs of Wales*, Brinley Richards wrote of the harp contest at the Llandovery Eisteddfod, expressing his pleasure at hearing several Welsh harpers, including a Welsh soldier,[51] in uniform, who played with 'remarkable skill.' He also commented on young Susanna Griffiths' performance:

The chief prize ... was a harp presented by Mr. Rees, of Tonn, ... The harp was won by a young Welsh girl, the daughter of the famous Gruffydd, domestic harper to Lady Llanover. She was dressed in the Welsh costume and her picturesque appearance and her very clever playing created enthusiasm.

Susanna married Edwin William Richards, an ironmonger, in July 1878, and they went to live in Abergavenny. Sadly Edwin died of typhoid fever just over a year later with his pregnant wife at his side and not long afterwards, on 15th December 1879, their son Edwin William Gruffydd[52] was born at *Tŷ'r Eglwys* [Church House], Lower Llanover. The 1881 census return shows Thomas Gruffydd and his wife Elizabeth, with their widowed daughter Su-

sanna and her one-year-old son, living at Church Farm, Llanover. After her father's death in 1887 Susanna became harper to Lady Llanover.

Ivor Herbert, Lady Llanover's eldest grandson, celebrated his 21st birthday in 1872 and he was given a brooch, or badge, of the finest quality. 'No expense was spared in employing the finest craftsmanship and using the most generous gauge of silver when making this badge.' It was just two inches in diameter, and decorated with Ivor Herbert's initials, leeks, and a Welsh Motto - *Asgre Lân Diogel Ei Pherchen* [A pure

Ivor Herbert's Badge

Image reproduced by kind permission of Sanda Lipton

---

51 Probably Sergeant W. Roberts, the Welsh Fusiliers, who won 2nd prize

52 Edwin William Griffith Richards. 1879-1930, was a member of the Welsh field hockey team that won a bronze medal in 1908 Olympic Games

conscience is a safeguard to its possessor]. It appears to be the type of expensive, Welsh-related gift that Lady Llanover would give, but there is no proof that this is so. The following year Ivor married Albertina Agnes Mary Denison, daughter of the deceased Lord Londesborough[53] and his wife Ursula Grace,[54] who had married Lord Otho Fitzgerald[55] after the death of her first husband. The marriage took place on the 31st July 1873 at the church of St Martin-in-the-Fields. *The Morning Post* reported the occasion in great detail. The bride wore a dress of rich white satin and the bridesmaids, among them Betha Johnes, wore dresses of white tarlatan over white silk. The numerous distinguished guests included the German Ambassador, the Earl of Powis and members of the Bunsen family. Also present were Col. Lyne, Lady Llanover's agent, and Mr A. J. Ram. The wedding ring was made of Welsh gold from Mr Johnes' mines at Dolaucothi, and was inscribed with the Welsh motto, *Y Gwir yn erbyn y Byd* [The Truth against the World]. The bridesmaids received solid gold lockets from the groom, which bore the initials of Col. Herbert and his bride in 'Welsh bardic characters' in the Llanarth colours of red and gold. On the reverse were inscribed the details of the occasion in both Welsh and English. The young couple received many presents, including beautiful jewellery and lace items; their gift from Lady Llanover was a Georgian carriage. The wedding breakfast was held at Lord and Lady Otho Fitzgerald's residence in Carlton House Terrace, where nearly 100 guests were accommodated in the spacious dining room.

What should have been a truly happy occasion was, however, somewhat marred. According to *The Morning Post* …

> *It was intended and had been fully arranged that the ceremony should have been performed at the Roman Catholic Oratory, at Brompton, as well as at St Martin's Church, and the bride's family and friends were all prepared to attend, but yesterday morning it having been discovered that the necessary license [sic] had not been procured for the Roman Catholic ceremony, it could not be then obtained. In consequence of the omission no marriage at the Oratory could take place, which announcement reached Carlton-house-terrace yesterday morning. The bridegroom's relatives, as Roman Catholics, did not, therefore, attend either the Protestant ceremony or the breakfast.*

The following day a letter from W. A. Johnson, Archbishop's House, West-

53 Lord Londesborough, Albert Denison, 1805-1860. m. Ursula Grace (née Bridgeman)

54 Ursula Grace Denison (née Bridgeman) – 1823-1883

55 Otho Fitzgerald, 1827-1882

minster, appeared in the same newspaper in response to the report of the wedding. Mr Johnson wished to correct the impression given by the newspaper that the only obstacle to a double religious ceremony had been the lack of a civil licence. He stressed that even if the necessary civil licence had been obtained the double ceremony still could not have taken place, and he quoted the Church's teaching:

> ... when the State recognises no marriage that does not take place before a Protestant Minister, and when therefore the Protestant minister may in such respect be regarded as a civil officer, Catholics may lawfully go through a form of marriage in his presence, for the purpose of obtaining legal validity for their union.

He went on to say that no such legal requirement had existed in England for many years, therefore the marriage of a Catholic before a Protestant minister was 'grievously wrong', as it was 'a participation in the religious rites of the Protestant religion, and "an implicit adhesion to heresy."' He went on to emphasise that Col. Herbert had been told, in no uncertain terms, that unless he gave his assurance that the Catholic ceremony would be the only marriage ceremony, then the marriage could not take place in a Catholic church. It is impossible to imagine the anguish of the occasion, which must have led to angry words on all sides. Two of the guests, both close friends of Lady Llanover and the Herberts, commiserated with each other on the difficult situation. In a letter to Betha Johnes written shortly after the event, Mr Ram mentioned his sympathy for both Llanover and Llanarth which 'would be so pleasant but so dangerous to express to both sides.' He could understand both sides of the argument and was 'greatly pained and grieved' by the state of affairs between the two families. He felt for Lady Llanover, who although 'appearing harsh and unyielding ... her every action springs from the desire to benefit those whom she is obliged to oppose.' Also he felt for the Herberts, although he could not begin to understand the 'overwhelming power of authority the conscientious fears – the absolute necessity by which they are constrained'. They were being asked to 'abandon for their descendants that which they hold to be vitally essential for themselves'. If they did that, would it be said that the motive was the hope of gaining wealth? What a conflict of duties faced her Ladyship's two granddaughters! On the one hand their religion and love for their parents, and on the other hand all that they owed to 'the kindest and most self sacrificing of grandmothers.' But in Ivor's case, how could one judge him? Added to his sisters' dilemma was his honour!

... honour as opposed to love, duty, conscience! nay it seems even as if honour were opposed to honour – for if a man gives a binding promise must he not in honour say if he finds that he cannot carry it out?[56]

Was Lady Llanover asking her grandchildren to forsake their religion and bring their children up as Protestants? Mr Ram hoped to hear that the unhappy situation was improving, and that 'hasty words or warm feelings were but the momentary result of misunderstanding or disappointment.'

Her Ladyship's granddaughter, Florence Herbert,[57] married Joseph Monteith[58] on 13th October 1874. The marriage took place in the small, private chapel at Llanarth. The bride was 'the daughter of a venerable and venerated house, and beloved ... for her own amiable characteristics.'[59] The day of the wedding was gloomy, with heavy clouds darkening the sky, but the threatening rain stayed away. The bride, regarded with affection by all who knew her, wore a dress of white satin and Brussels lace, trimmed with flowers, and on her head a wreath of orange blossoms. The bridesmaids' dresses were of light mauve silk, with tunics of creamy-white figured silk, trimmed with mauve feathers. Among the bridesmaids were Miss Herbert, of Llanarth[60] and Miss Tozer,[61] her cousin. The Right Rev. Dr Brown, Roman Catholic Bishop of Newport and Menevia, conducted the service and the Rev. Edmund de la Rue, Chaplain of Llanarth, said the wedding mass. Afterwards the bells of the parish church 'rang out merry peals' and guns were fired to celebrate the occasion. A magnificent breakfast had been prepared at the mansion, following which the newly-weds left for Ross 'amidst the heartiest demonstrations of respect and affection'. There were numerous costly gifts among which was a set of ornaments made of Mocha stones[62] from Lady Llanover. Thankfully the day seems to have passed happily with none of the controversy that attended the marriage of Ivor Herbert.

Although her Ladyship has been described as 'a bull-dozer of a woman',[63] and she certainly was a very determined woman, she had a softer side, as is shown by her care for family and friends who were ill. In an undated memo

---

56 NLW Dolaucothi papers L9011
57 Florence Herbert, 1850-1900
58 Joseph Monteith, 1852-1911
59 *The Western Mail*
60 Henrietta Herbert, 1848-? Florence's sister
61 Miss Tozer – probably Henrietta, 1857-?, daughter of John Hillier Tozer and Mary Louise (née Herbert)
62 Mocha - a precious stone fashionable in the mid-eighteenth century for jewellery
63 Eiry Hunter, Welsh Folk Dance Society

to Dafydd Williams she shows her fondness for nature's creatures:

You must examine again very soon about the jackdaws, but it would have been enough to bring a Judgement upon us if the Old Birds had been barred out from coming to feed the Young ones before the young ones could take care of themselves but they made such a noise today in Church that Mr. Bevan says he is sure they must have been hatched some of them - under the Tiles between the Tiles & the Ceiling in the body of the Church when the little Jackdaws are fledged before they can fly away is the time when those that are fond of them take them to rear & I should think by the Chatter they made over my pew today in Church that there must be some & it would be no Cruelty to take to rear – but be that as it may the place must not be stopped until they are provided for by flying away or somebody wishing to have them to Nurse I don't want to have one here now as there is enough to do & no one to care for it when I am gone to London but John Evans use to rear them formerly & as they eat worms they are not expensive to keep.[64]

It is said that she was also concerned about the horses labouring up the long slope from Llanellen to Rhydymeirch, and around 1875 she had a horse trough built which has around its edge the inscription 'YFWCH BAWB A CHROESAW AC NAC ANGHOF-IWCH WENYNEN GWENT' [Drink, all, and welcome, and do not for-get Gwenynen Gwent]. There are also three Welsh verses, one of which translates as fol-lows:

The Horse Trough at Llanover
Photograph: Terry Evans

Water, O Lord, is the drink
When you would allow us to refresh our tongues
The Devil sent alcohol
To put an end to man and his wealth.[65]

---

64 GRO D.1210.1505

65 *A Gazeteer of Monmouthshire Wellsites*

The many vehicles rushing along the busy road through Rhydymeirch today would scarcely notice the trough, let alone be able to stop and read the words!

Betha Johnes' father, John Johnes, was at one time county court judge for the counties of Carmarthen, Cardigan and Pembroke. He was a highly respected man who lived at the family seat, Dolaucothi[66] with his two daughters, Charlotte and Betha. Charlotte was the widow of Captain Charles Cookman.[67] The butler at Dolaucothi was an Irishman, Henry Tremble, who had been Captain Cookman's valet and general servant. He was eighteen years old when he first came to Dolaucothi with Captain and Mrs Cookman, and after Captain Cookman's death he worked in the stables at Dolaucothi, eventually becoming coachman. After the death of Mr Johnes' personal servant he made the Irishman his butler. Tremble married the daughter of a local farmer, but the marriage was a stormy one, he being a very jealous man. Following a short, unsuccessful spell keeping the Sexton's Inn in Caio, Tremble went to live at Dolaucothi, but his wife and children lived in a house in Caio, a couple of miles away.

For some time, Henry Tremble had wanted the tenancy at the Dolaucothi Arms, which belonged to Mr Johnes, who must have been aware of weaknesses in Tremble's character because he would not accede to his butler's frequent requests. The resentment building up inside Tremble finally came to a head and he gave Mr Johnes a month's notice to quit his position in the household. On the day his notice expired[68] he performed his usual duties, although he was unusually quiet. In the mid-morning Mr Johnes was in his study, when Tremble burst in. Without saying a word, he left again, only to return within a few seconds carrying a gun. Still saying nothing, he raised the gun and shot Mr Johnes. Leaving the study he went to the kitchen where he found Mrs Cookman speaking to the cook. 'You and Miss Johnes', he said,

The Dolaucothi Arms/Hotel

---

66   Near Llandovery, Carms

67   Captain Charles Cookman of Enniscothy, co. Wexford. ? – 1866?

68   19th August 1876

133

'have always been against me. You have always been my enemies. I'll pay you', and, pointing the gun at the frightened lady, he shot her too. Lady Wilkinson, who was a guest at Dolaucothi at the time, heard the shot and rushed to the study where she found Mr Johnes, mortally wounded. He was able to tell her that it was Tremble who had shot him, but within the hour the unfortunate man died. Tremble reloaded his gun and made his way to the kennels where he called the dogs out and one by one he shot them too. Eventually the wretched man reached his home,[69] went upstairs, and after some exchanges with the policemen outside, he shot himself. 'Thus cheating justice of her due.'[70] Meanwhile Charlotte's wounds were being treated, and although they were serious, it was hoped that she would survive. Three days later, at the Wrexham Eisteddfod,[71] the whole assembly was asked to stand to express their deep sympathy with the Johnes family.[72]

David Morris, *Eiddil Gwent*,[73] was a writer of poetry, prose and song. He won first prize at the Tredegar Cymmrodorion Society Eisteddfod of 1862 with his *History of Tredegar* which was published in 1868. In spite of his success he ended his days in the Tredegar workhouse. Lady Llanover held him in great respect and was very kind to him, especially in his later years, sending him a pound every New Year's Day. After his death some friends began collecting money to erect a monument over his grave, and knowing of Lady Llanover's generosity, approached her for a donation. She wrote back to them with very little ceremony to the effect that they should have done more for him when he was alive, but she would give something after she had seen the total amount collected.[74]

Bridget Dafydd was living in Llanover at this time. She was the sister of Elizabeth Davis, *Betsy Cadwaladr*, the Balaclava nurse, whose story was written by Jane Williams, *Ysgafell*. Their father was Dafydd Cadwaladr of Bala, a friend of Thomas Charles[75] of Bala. Elizabeth changed her name to Davis 'because of the "murdering" of Cadwaladr by English-speaking folk.' Bridget had lived in London for many years, in the service of Lord and Lady Llanover and in her old age she must have returned to Llanover, where she died on

---

69 Myrtle Cottage, Caio

70 NLW Charlotte Johnes' diary

71 Wrexham Eisteddfod, 22nd-25th August 1876

72 *Y Cymmrodor*

73 David Morris, *Eiddil Gwent*, c. 1798-1878

74 *Memoirs of William Williams (Myfyr Wyn)*, Blaenau Gwent website.

75 Thomas Charles of Bala, 1755-1814

21st March, 1878, at the age of 83. Throughout her life she was a faithful member of the Calvinistic Methodists and she is buried at Capel Ed, Goytre.[76]

One Llanover carpenter and harp maker of note was Abraham Jeremiah. Abraham had been a favourite of Lady Llanover but she did not approve of his marriage, in 1868, to Elizabeth Harris, a publican's daughter, and following the wedding her attitude towards him cooled rather[77] but she still wanted him to make triple harps! A memo dated 8th June 1880, initialled by Lady Llanover, reads as follows:

A Welsh harp is ordered for Abram [sic] to finish off for a friend of Mr Brinley Richards. My Lady wishes you to write the account out as soon as it is ready and enclose it to my Lady all ready for Post, ... she hopes that you will see [the harp] is securely packed as if it is damaged on the road it would not be paid for. The Gentleman who has ordered it is a very good Musician and anxious to have a good Welsh Harp and very likely he would write a description of it in some Book, & so Abram must be very careful that it is on the real Welsh model which he has always had to Copy & get Gruffydd to try it & string it that he may know all is right.

The order was placed on the 8th June, the harp was despatched to Carl Engel in London on 2nd July, its safe arrival was acknowledged on 6th July, together with a cheque made out to Abraham Jeremiah for £11, and the receipt for the cheque was signed by Abraham on 7th July. Less than one month to construct, string and test a triple harp, make a strong container for it, arrange its safe delivery to London and receive and acknowledge payment! He also made a harp for Harry Parry of Holyhead.[78] For this he received a cheque for £11.11.6, which was sent to him care of Mrs Williams, Housekeeper, Llanover.

In 1881, Abraham and his wife and children were living at the Carpenters Arms, the present Goytre Arms, with his father-in-law John Harris, publican and carpenter. It seems that John Harris was also the local undertaker and it is said that the coffins were kept in the cellar of the pub![79] After Abraham's death from cancer in 1886 his wife ran the public house, and in 1891 she was living there with her daughter Mary and her two sons, Thomas and John, both carpenters. Mary later married Franklin Harris of Gwenffrwd, and in 1901 he was innkeeper at the Carpenters Arms, living with Mary his wife,

---

76 *Calvinistic Methodist History Society Magazine*
77 Story from a descendant of Abraham Jeremiah
78 Harry Parry, *Ty Rhosedd*, Penrhos, Holyhead GRO D1210.821
79 Story from a descendant of Abraham Jeremiah

their daughter Mary and his brother-in-law John Jeremiah.

At least one harp made by Abraham travelled much further than London. It belonged to the Rev. Michael D. Jones[80] of Bala whose sons, Mihangel ap Iwan and Llwyd ap Iwan, had been taught to play the instrument by *Gruffydd* when they were children in Llanover. He considered it to be the best harp in Llanover at the time. The harp is now in the Museo Historico Regional in Gaiman, Patagonia, having been rescued, in 1899, from the worst flood in the Chubut Valley since the first Welsh people had arrived there in 1865. It was then sent by ship to Buenos Aires, to the home of Dr Mihangel ap Iwan where it remained for many years before being returned to Chubut. Sadly it now has no strings – one of Dr Mihangel's grandsons was heard to own up to stealing some of its strings to make a bow and arrow![81]

Harp made by Abraham Jeremiah now in Patagonia

Photograph: Catrin Junyent

Writing about Lady Llanover in his book, *The South Wales Squires*, H. M. Vaughan[82] states:

Like most aliens of a fanatical nature, Lady Llanover ruthlessly inflicted her new fad on all and sundry. As the countryside around Llanover was wholly anglicized, she met this difficulty by importing a number of monoglot Welsh-speaking Methodists from North Cardiganshire.

One such Welsh-speaking Methodist from Cardiganshire was David Williams[83] from Aberystwyth. He began his working life as a joiner and by the time he reached Llanover, about 1882/3, he was an architect! One of his sons, Griffith, was born in Aberystwyth in October 1882, but it is probable

---

80 Rev. Michael Daniel Jones, 1822-1898

81 My thanks to Ms Tegai Roberts for the information

82 Herbert Millingchanp Vaughan, 1870-1948

83 David Williams, 1834-1924; the author's great grandfather

that by then David Williams was already in Llanover. He was certainly not a monoglot Welsh speaker, as is shown in some of his letters written to, and on behalf of, Lady Llanover. In Llanover he and his family lived in the former

Nightingale Inn in Pengroes-oped, which Lady Llanover had bought and made into a home for the Williams family. The house was named *Tŷ Eos Y Coed*, [House of the Nightingale in the Wood] and David Williams became Mr Dafydd Williams, under-agent! Dafydd and his wife spoke English and Welsh, as did their children.

Tŷ Eos Y Coed (formerly The Nightingale Inn)

Before the family left Aberystwyth two of the children had died of scarlet fever on the same day! George, aged four, and Mary Ann, two, died on 18th April, 1881. Not long after the family had settled in Llanover Dafydd suffered another loss; on 20th December 1883 his eldest child, Margaret Jane,[84] was 'found dead' from natural causes, according to the inquest. She was twenty-one years old and is buried in the shade of a yew tree in the churchyard at St Bartholomew's. The following items appear in Dafydd Williams's account book:

Monthly payments due 5th January 1884

Cards printed in Welsh for Coffin Inscription	*1s.0d*
Dafydd Morris, Digging Grave	*7s.0d*

Although her name is not mentioned, it is possible that this was for Margaret Jane. A year later Dafydd and his wife had another daughter, and it was Lady Llanover who gave her the name *Eos Mwynwen*.

When Lady Llanover was in London she liked to be kept informed of how things were in Llanover. In April 1884 she wrote to Mr Dafydd Williams regarding the Dressing of the Graves for *Dydd Sadwrn y Blodau* [probably *Dydd Sul y Blodau* -Palm Sunday]. In the letter she wrote:

You are welcome to ask Davies Yr Ardd[85] for some little sprigs of Laurel which would [look] very pretty pegged down around your Poor Daughter's Grave

---

84 Margaret Jane Williams, 1862-1883, daughter of David Williams and his first wife Elizabeth Richards
85 Davies the Garden

and there are quantities of Daf-
fodils growing in many fields of
farms where I am sure they
would let you have some and
there used to be a quantity at
Llwyn Celyn – If you do not get
them overnight or by daylight
in the morning others will be
sure to get them.[86]

The grave of Margaret Jane Williams

That year her Ladyship lost yet another of her faithful servants. Mary Manuel, mother of those amazing young boys who died so tragically young, died at the age of eighty. She had been a widow for fifteen years, and had outlived all her children except Freeman Manuel, who was a preacher in Australia. She had lived in Llanover for many years and was noted for her intelligence, her love of Wales, her warmth and her steadfast support of the Temperance Movement. She had taught her children the Welsh language, at which she excelled, and had brought them up to be respectful to the people they knew.

In the early 1880s there was a young man named Gwilym Griffiths living and working in Llanover who seems to have been discontented with his lot. In 1883 he was in Lady Llanover's service as a groom, being paid at the rate of thirteen shillings a week.

6th October 1883 - Gwilym Gryffydd –   *5 weeks @ 13/- £3. 5. 0.*
ditto arrears   *5 weeks @ 3/-   15. 0.*

By August 1884 he must have persuaded her Ladyship that he was worth more and from then on he was paid at the rate of fourteen shillings a week, with the extra shilling being backdated for seventeen weeks!

---

86 GRO D1210.1497

2nd August 1884 – Gwilym Griffiths – 4 weeks   *@ 13/-*
ditto 17 weeks extra as promised by her Ladyship   *@ 1/-*[87]

This seems to have satisfied young Gwilym for a while; the next notable entry for him in Dafydd Williams's account book is nearly three years later. On March 5th 1887 he was paid for one week only at fourteen shillings, probably his final pay before he emigrated to America.

Poor Gwilym! He just could not cope with life in Pennsylvania. Fortunately there was a family friend, Mr T. Foulkes, who looked after him. William, as he became known, had been very badly affected by the news of his brother Harry's death. He had taken to his bed for a week and Mr and Mrs Foulkes cared for him night and day. He would not eat or drink, thinking that it would kill him. The doctor thought he would be better off in hospital so he was there for five weeks during which time Mr and Mrs Foulkes visited him regularly. William then decided that he wanted to leave hospital, and as they could not keep him there it was decided to send him to the Danville State Hospital for the Insane. On the 18th June 1887 Dr Schultz[88] wrote to Mr Foulkes:

Dear Sir,

William Griffiths has not changed any since he came here with the exception that he now takes nourishment readily and in sufficient amount when it is put to his mouth. He has also eaten a little himself, but not enough. At first he had to be urged, almost forced, to take sufficient food. He also takes his medicine, but still prefers to stand about with his head down and says hardly anything that is intelligible or plainly audible. I trust that in a few weeks or a month more, we may be able to report some more decided change for the better.

I would not look for much improvement in so short a time. He is in a quiet ward and I think he is as comfortable as his mental condition permits him to be made.

Very Truly Yours,

S. S. Schultz

Less than two weeks later, Mr Foulkes received another report about William. This time the letter was signed by H. B. Meredith, Assistant Physician. There had been 'no material change' in William's condition. Eating was still a problem, but he was getting 'about sufficient nourishment.' He seemed

---

87 GRO D1210.1311.

88 Dr Soloman S. Schultz, first Superintendent of Danville State Hospital

'entirely taken up with his melancholy delusions' and Dr Meredith thought it would do no good for him to have visitors. Mr Foulkes was sufficiently worried about William's condition to write to his mother suggesting that someone should travel to America to 'fetch him from here that he may get well again.'

We will do all we can for him but I think the best remedy would be for you to come yourself – if it is possible – to fetch him that he may get allright [sic] by crossing the water.

He told Mrs Griffiths that he heard weekly from the doctor and intended to visit William soon, and he enclosed two letters from the hospital for her to read herself. Shortly after the family received Mr Foulkes' letter, William's married sister, Ann Howell, who lived in Cardiff, took matters into her own hands. She wrote a letter to Lady Llanover with a heartfelt plea for her advice.

I Ann Howell ... do take the liberty of writing to Her Ladyship in the hopes that we will gain thereby Her Ladyship's advice ... I hope Her Ladyship will pardon us for troubling her ... if it is not too much to ask I pray that Her Ladyship will listen to this.

And her Ladyship's response?

Mr Dafydd Williams,
Since writing my last letter I have rec'd enclosed most extraordinary application to ask me to help bring Gwilym back. What fools they must be ... to apply to me of all people ... It makes it clear what harm he has done himself – going to **America** [89]

Dafydd Williams wrote to Ann Howell ...

As instructed by the Right Honourable Lady Llanofer I wish to return to you the letters which were sent to her Ladyship. Her Ladyship is away from home at the moment – but she had your letters. Her Ladyship wishes me to tell you that she can only say that Gwilym Gruffydd had every advice not to go to **America,** *but he would not listen to reason, and he left her Ladyship's service with a fortnight's notice. Her Ladyship thinks it will not be wise to bring him home unless he has returned to his senses – therefore her Ladyship is not able to judge who will be best to bring him home. Her Ladyship is very sorry for his mother and hopes she will advise his brother John (who is at present in her service) to be a good boy and also to appreciate the kindness shown to him by*

---

89 GRO D1210.822.1

Her Ladyship.[90]

Poor Mrs Griffiths! She had been a widow for many years and now Harry, her soldier son, had died and another son was in a mental institution thousands of miles away. Her married daughter was living in Cardiff, and she herself was unable to earn much money following an accident to her right arm.

There are also many documents showing Lady Llanover's kindness towards her tenants. At the beginning of July 1884 Mary Walters was paid four shillings for 'washing and airing' *Bwthyn Pen yr Heol* [Cottage at the top of the road].[91] On the 19th July, Ann Morgan wrote a letter of thanks to Her Ladyship.

I, Ann Morgan, widow of the late Stonemason,[92] feel humble and truly thankful from my heart to the Right Honourable Lady Llanover for continuing her kindness towards me and my little children[93] by allowing me to have the garden produce, namely the fruit and vegetables this year - and I will do my best to fulfil my Lady's order through caring for the garden.[94]

In a letter to Dafydd Williams, sent from London in April 1884, Lady Llanover had enquired about what work had been done in the garden at *Bwthyn Pen yr Heol*. Was she already planning to let the bereaved Morgan family live there?

In September 1887, young Thomas Morgan, aged nine, died of 'Acute Dispepsia'. By 1891 Ann Morgan, her three surviving sons and her daughter Blodwen were living in Rhydymeirch, and daughter Charlotte was a general servant at Ty Uchaf.

On the 1st August 1885 Ann Watkins was paid two pounds five shillings for working for five weeks at the Vicarage. On the 5th August Lady Llanover wrote to Mr Dafydd Williams:

About Gwynionydd.[95] If he likes to go and settle in the Vicerdy [Vicarage] on **Saturday next** *please tell him from the Arglwyddes[96] he is* **welcome to do so** *but that he had better have his dinner at the Ty-Uchaf first . . . Tell Mrs.*

---

90 GRO D1210.822.1. Translated from the original Welsh by the author
91 Dafydd Williams A/c book GRO D1210.1311
92 Henry Morgan, died January 1884 of stomach cancer
93 John, Charlotte, Thomas, David, Henry and Blodwen (who was born after her father's death)
94 GRO D1210. Translated from the original Welsh by the author
95 Rev. Benjamin Williams *Gwynionydd 1821-1891*
96 By this time Lady Llanover was referred to by her tenants as the *Arglwyddes* - the Lady

*Evan Jones the above and that the Arglwyddes has no time to write to her -
but that she and Mrs. Chubb are to send for Ann Watkins up to tell her what
Gwynionydd is to take and how to cook everything for him. Mr. D. W. is to let
Ann Watkins have the use of a Ffwrn fach [little oven] and one Double besides – & a gridiron instead of the Frying Pan she now has – She must not fry
anything for him it is bad for his health.*[97]

In her unusual 'cookery book' Lady Llanover writes of her preference for
the Double over the Bain-Marie.

*The reader ... who may possibly be acquainted with the copper tray called a
Bain-Marie, to hold hot water, which is used by professed cooks to keep their
sauces from burning, and may probably suppose that that contrivance was **unknown** to the Hermit, and that his system of double vessels for cookery was
only a clumsy substitution for a scientific invention, beyond his knowledge or
his reach; it is, therefore, necessary to add, that it was in consequence of the
total **inefficiency** of the copper tray, called a Bain-Marie, to effect the objects
which it was the ambition of the Hermit to attain, that he discarded the Bain-
Marie altogether, as an expensive and cumbersome addition to his kitchen,
which took up a great deal of room, and did very little work, and was totally
inadmissible where there was not a very large stove.*

The town of Caerwys, in Flintshire, is 'rich in eisteddfodic associations'[98]
which date back many centuries, to the year 1100, when *Gruffydd ap Cynan*[99]
ordered a meeting to be held to 'revise, amend, and improve the twenty-four
musical canons.' Several 'bardic festivals' were held in the following years,
but by 1568 'a long period of anarchy had existed amongst the bards' so
Queen Elizabeth appointed a commission to organise an eisteddfod at Caerwys 'to advance the ingenious and skilful to the accustomed degrees, and to
restore to the graduates their ancient exclusive privilege of exercising their
profession.' None of the succeeding monarchs convened such a meeting, but
in 1798 the London Gwyneddigion Society obtained 'extensive and respectable patronage' for an eisteddfod to be held in Caerwys.

Nearly 100 years later, in 1886, a truly Welsh eisteddfod was held at Caerwys, the object being to rescue 'the Welsh eisteddfod from its present foreign
and Anglican condition, and restoring to it its pristine honour.'[100] Lord
Mostyn,[101] whose ancestor, William Mostyn, was one of Queen Elizabeth's

---

97 GRO D1210.1498
98 *The Flintshire Observer*
99 *Gruffydd ap Cynan* - 11th/12th century King of Gwynedd
100 *The Flintshire Observer*
101 Llewelyn Nevill Vaughan Lloyd-Mostyn, 3rd Baron, 1856-1929

commissioners, fully supported the event, and was president of the General Committee. At the Eisteddfod he wore the Mostyn Silver Harp, the ancient 'badge of honour' which had been 'in the gift of the Mostyn family from time immemorial.' The badge, or brooch, measures about six inches long and has nine strings, which represent the nine muses, and Lord Mostyn gave a replica to the Eisteddfod to be presented to the best *pennillion*[102] singer.

The promoters of the Eisteddfod entitled it 'The Royal Welsh Eisteddfod of Wales, the chair of Arthur and co-efficient Gorsedd of the Bards of the Isle of Britain', and different to the Royal National Eisteddfod, which will be held at Carnarvon the week after next, inasmuch as it is exclusively Welsh, the use of English being studiously avoided.[103]

The Denbighshire Free Press stressed how different the 'Royal Welsh Eisteddfod of Wales ...' would be from the 'Royal National Eisteddfod which will be held at Carnarvon the week after next, inasmuch as it is exclusively Welsh, the use of English being studiously avoided.'

This must have been music to Lady Llanover's ears, and it was she who arranged the rules for the harp competitions. No one could compete who had played the pedal harp ...

... the object being to restore to its proper position the national instrument of the principality, and to encourage the cultivation of the pure and simple style in which ancient Welsh music ought to be played.

An excerpt from *The Flintshire Observer* reads as follows:

In order to encourage the use of the Welsh Harp as the domestic instrument of the Principality, Lady Llanover (Gwenynen Gwent), gave very handsome prizes for competition, besides sending over at her own expense, Gruffydd

Elizabeth Ann Williams, aged 16, at the Caerwys Eisteddfod 1886

---

102 *Pennillion* - literally verses of a song or hymn
103 *The Denbighshire Free Press*

(harper by special appointment to the Prince of Wales and the Llanover family), and his pupils.

Among these pupils was Dafydd Williams's young daughter, Elizabeth Ann.[104] She was sixteen years old and had begun to play the harp, under *Gruffydd's* tuition, just two months earlier. She played *Merch Megan* and won the first prize of three pounds, which had been given by Lord Tredegar. The adjudicator of the harp competitions was Dr Joseph Parry, at that time Principal of the Musical College of Wales, Swansea. A choir from Swansea attended the Eisteddfod ...

Dr Joseph Parry

'... *at the expense of Lady Llanover, in recognition of the fact that the eisteddfod was to be conducted purely in Welsh ... In order to keep in harmony with the Welsh sentiment which animated Lady Llanover, the ladies of the choir were attired in Welsh costumes ...* [105]

The main harp competition at the eisteddfod was won by Thomas Gruffydd's daughter, Susanna Gruffydd Richards. The tune was *Penrhaw* and her mark was ninety-three out of a possible one hundred. She received ten pounds and a gold medal, which had the Prince of Wales feathers on one side and a representation of the Welsh harp and Welsh emblematic leek on the other, the medal having been given by Lady Llanover. Lord Tredegar had given extra prizes and she received another three pounds from him. Although later known as *Pencerddes y De*, at this eisteddfod her pseudonym was *Twynwen*.

As well as the Swansea choir's expenses, Lady Llanover had given the Llanover party two bankers orders amounting to £120. Their costs were as follows:-

---

104 The author's grandmother, Elizabeth Ann Williams, 1870-1956

105 *The Flintshire Observer*

Railway Carriage for seven	£7.16. 2
Robert McKirdy to Bala	5. 6
Telegrams	4. 4
Rev. E. Bevan - costs in Caerwys	2. 5. 0
Rev. T. C. Phillips, Abercarn, costs in Caerwys	2.10. 0
A Total of	£13. 1. 0

Their board and lodging was paid for by the Secretary of the Committee, as was the cost of conveying the harps from the station to the town. Prizes amounting to £49.10.0 were given, and after all costs had been deducted the balance of £57. 9. 0 was returned to her Ladyship on the 4th October.

It was sad that Brinley Richards had died the previous year, at the age of 67. However, his contribution towards 'saving' the national instrument was not forgotten – an image of a Welsh triple-stringed harp was carved on his gravestone.

Brinley Richards' Grave
Photographs: Iain MacFarlaine

A young man who won a prize at that eisteddfod was Edward Davies, *Taibach*. He had been given a scholarship by Lady Llanover after coming to Llanover to have an audition with *Gruffydd*. A letter from her Ladyship's London home at Great Stanhope Street, Mayfair, to Mr. Rhys Morgan, Secretary of the Committee at Taibach, reads as follows:

I am directed by the Right Honble Lady Llanover to say that she has this day received your letter saying that you will send the "Boy" whose name you have

omitted to mention, to Gruffydd next Saturday for trial. Her Ladyship is sorry
that you have written to Gruffydd before you informed her of this, but she hopes
that he will receive the letter which she sends him by this post before he receives
yours, as he will not at all understand that Her Ladyship either took interest
in the Boy or would authorise his being sent to him on trial without previous
explanation from herself ... The Boy's visit to Llanover on Saturday next would
enable him to make acquaintance with Mr Dafydd Williams her Under Agent
and also her Housekeeper and several religious people in her immediate service,
who would take an interest in him & see that his Sunday was properly spent
& that he had good companions.
signed E. Francis.[106]

Following his visit, Edward was given a very hopeful report by *Gruffydd*, and his scholarship began on 1st of June that same year, 1884. The conditions were 'To find himself in Lodging & food – & have his Scholarship renewed every Quarter for One Year, if deserving & well conducted or otherwise dismissal.' *Gruffydd* and Her Ladyship must have been well pleased with young Edward Davies at the Caerwys Eisteddfod in 1886 – he gained the full number of 100 marks for his playing of *Pant Corlan yr Wyn*.

Another young man who received a harp scholarship from Lady Llanover was Pedr [Peter] James. In February 1888 his mother, the widowed Elizabeth James, and Lady Llanover signed the necessary agreements. Lady Llanover, for the one part, agreed to give Pedr a trial of three months with Mrs Gruffydd Richards, who had taken on her father's position after his death the previous year. If Pedr showed willing to learn, he could continue for another term – if there was nothing to be said against him! For the other part, Elizabeth James acknowledged that the triple harp already in her house belonged to Lady Llanover, and that if Pedr was given a scholarship the harp would be loaned to him for him to practise; but she would return the harp at any time, if that was what Her Ladyship wished. The harp was already in Mrs James' possession because her son John, *Ioan ab Ioan*, had been learning to play the harp. Elizabeth's husband, John James senior, was a general labourer who died of smallpox in 1872, at the age of 42, leaving his widow with four children, John junior, James, Peter and Arthur. In attendance at the death was Susanna Griffiths, probably the daughter of *Gruffydd*, the harper. At the time, Susanna Griffiths would have been about eighteen years of age, John junior seven, James

---

106 Elizabeth Francis, sister of Elias Francis, harp maker

six, Peter three and Arthur just eight months old. Eliza Ann James, another child, had died in 1867 *yn ei mabandod* [in her infancy].

The census for 1881 shows Elizabeth James, a thirty-eight-year-old widow, living at Yew Tree Cottage with her two sons Peter aged 11 and Arthur aged 9. The 1881 census shows a James James, aged 15, born in Llanover, under-gardener at Ty Uchaf.

In the under-agent's account book, there is an entry dated May 1883, showing Elizabeth James being paid at the rate of 2/6 a week for cleaning the schoolroom. At the time, the schoolmistress was Rachel Evans. She and her husband John Elias Evans lived in the School House, Llanover. In 1881 John Elias Evans's occupation was under-butler, but by 1891 he was a gardener. He was also a harper and had played his triple harp before Queen Victoria at the Royal Albert Hall. His daughter Elizabeth Lilian, who was born at Llanover School House, inherited the harp, and it was her wish that it be given to Abergavenny Museum. That same account book has an entry dated August 1885 for Arthur ab Ioan's book – Arthur James that is – £1 4s. 0. but no indication as to the nature of his work. On the 1891 census he gives his occupation as 'Clerk at Iron Works'.

John Elias Evans' Harp

Image reproduced by kind permission of Monmouthshire County Council, Abergavenny Museum

Part of a letter written by Lady Llanover in 1884 to her agent Dafydd Williams reads as follows:-

Dr Harper says Ab Ioan if as well as when I saw him on Tuesday may go a little into the Garden if not too cold if Davies could give him light work ...... & put it down by the hour - he cannot attempt days work nor going out early in the cold but hours will make days and he may gain a little and the air is good for him after he has had his dinner when the weather permits.

Poor young John suffered from tuberculosis and died on St. David's Day, 1886.

When James Williams, one of Dafydd Williams's sons, reached the age of fourteen he began learning to play the harp under the tuition of Susanna Gruffydd Richards. One page in her account book[107] records the following:

To 1 month's instruction	
On Welsh harp	
To 3 scholarship	
pupils due 31st July	*£3. 3. 0*
To 6 lessons given	
to James Williams	
@ 2/6 per lesson	*15. 0*
Harp Strings	*7. 0*
	£4. 5. 0

Received with thanks
Aug. 19th 1889
S. B. Richards

Dafydd Williams

A few months later, the Williams family moved to Cardiff, probably due to the severe illness of Dafydd's wife, Mary, who died in 1902 after suffering from rheumatic arthritis for twelve years. Kelly's Directory for Monmouthshire and South Wales, 1895, records James Williams, Welsh Harpist, living in Cranbrook Street, Cardiff.

By the 1890s Lady Llanover had outlived nearly all her closest friends and had been a widow for over twenty years. In a letter to Betha Johnes, written when she was approaching her ninety-second birthday, she wrote, 'My heart sinks – really not a day passes without some melancholy event or something directly associated with one ... '[108] Of her three children, only her daughter, Mrs Herbert, survived.

Her Ladyship had remained fairly active, considering her great age, play-

---

107 GRO D.1210.494/495
108 *THSC* 'Lady Llanover and Her Circle', Maxwell Fraser.

ing her part as a trustee of Llandovery School and personally supervising the business of her estate – she insisted that she, herself, interviewed prospective tenant farmers. In an undated memo her Ladyship stated:

> *I will see the man about the Lapstone [Cottage] but I cannot call to mind what Thomas Morgan, he is but if he is a **Cymro** [Welshman] a good workman and a good character he might have work here ...* [109]

She visited Bath and London and stayed with friends and family, her faithful companion, Jane Ryder, by her side. She even attended a Welsh concert in London given by John Thomas, *Pencerdd Gwalia*, when 'Twenty harps played by Ladies in White' were heard. These were, no doubt, pedal harps!

Jane Ryder's appointment came about in what would appear to be typical Lady Llanover style! Maxwell Fraser wrote:

> *The last of Lady Llanover's companions was Miss Jane Ryder (1861-1950) of Ty Ucha', Llanwrin, Montgomery, where the Rev. D. Sylvan Evans was the Vicar. Lady Llanover asked him to find someone who could read Welsh to the children of the Marquess of Bute, but stipulated that she should first go to Llanover for her (Lady Llanover's) approval. Sylvan Evans, who was a friend of the Ryder family, suggested that Jane Ryder should apply for the post – but she never got further than Llanover. Lady Llanover took such a liking to her that she engaged her as her own companion.* [110]

For some months, her Ladyship had been unable to attend the services at the Calvinistic Methodist Church in Llanover, which previously she had done every Sunday, dressed in 'the orthodox Welsh costume.' The pastor, Rev. J. Prys, was Lady Llanover's chaplain, and frequently visited her at the *Llys*. He called one January day in 1896 and, as usual, ended his visit with a prayer. During his recent visits Lady Llanover had begun making quiet remarks during the prayers, asking the pastor 'to make certain appeals in consonance with her frame of mind at the time.' On this occasion she interrupted the prayers saying, '*Gweddiwch am gael i mi ffydd, amynedd, a nerth o dan brofedigaeth.* (Beseech that I may be given faith, patience, and strength in the day of trial.)' [111]

Her Ladyship had made arrangements to interview one of her prospective tenants on the following day. However, she was suffering from a very slight cold and stayed in bed. Dr Steele, of Abergavenny, called, as he did every day,

---

109 GRO D.1210.1505
110 *THSC* 'Lady Llanover and Her Circle', Maxwell Fraser
111 *The South Wales Daily News*

and saw no reason for concern. She had a light meal and then fell asleep, or so it was thought. Her maids were in the room at the time and became concerned when they realised that their beloved *Arglwyddes* was not sleeping, but had drifted into unconsciousness. They raised the alarm, summoned the Rev. Prys, then, peacefully, her frail body held gently in Jane Ryder's arms, the dear Lady finally left the home and the land she had loved so much.

Sketch of Lady Llanover
The Western Mail. Photograph: Moira Harry

> *Our beloved Arglwyddes Llanover breathed her last in my arms from 3 to 4 on Friday afternoon ...* [112]

Over a hundred years earlier, Augusta's talented and accomplished ancestor, Mrs Delany, said, 'I like, and love, and dislike with all my might.'[113] Her protégée, Augusta's equally talented and accomplished mother, Georgina Mary Anne (née Port), had exhorted her daughters, 'Whatever you do, do it with all your might.' Can it be denied that although two centuries separate the birth of the one and the death of the other, the influence of Mrs Delany, through her love and care for her great niece, Georgina Mary Anne, helped to form the character of that unique 'Welshwoman', *Gwenynen Gwent*, Augusta, Baroness Llanover?

---

112 *THSC* 'Lady Llanover and Her Circle', Maxwell Fraser

113 *Mrs Delany's Menus, Medicines and Manners*, Katherine Cahill

Chapter 6
Beyond the Grave

When [Lady Llanover] died, on the 17ᵗʰ January 1896 ... visitors to the place witnessed that a profound hiraeth and a feeling of loss was perceived throughout the Court.[1]

The traditional picture of Lady Llanover as an absolute autocrat, over-riding everyone, is so unattractive that if it were true it would be surprising that she had any friends at all.[2]

Messages bearing the sad news were sent immediately to Her Ladyship's family. Mrs Herbert and her sons, Ivor and Arthur, were in London, and her daughter[3] in Cannes. Her son Bleiddian[4] was already in Llanover although not in the mansion at the time of his grandmother's death. Ivor, then Commanding Officer of the 2nd Battalion, the Grenadier Guards at Chelsea Barracks, travelled from London to Newport that night, then drove on to Llanover. Mrs Herbert and Arthur, a member of the Diplomatic Corps, arrived the following day, as did Colonel Lyne, Lady Llanover's agent, and Mr A. J. Ram, her cousin who was a London barrister.

The funeral was held on the following Thursday[5] and was simple and unpretentious, in accordance with Her Ladyship's wishes. The whole proceedings were conducted in Welsh, the language she had always cherished.

The early morning storm clouds moved slowly away, leaving the surrounding hills shrouded in a mournful, grey mist. Crowded trains brought people to pay their respects and the roads were bustling with people on foot, on horseback and in carriages, all heading to Llanover.

They mourned the loss of a considerate landowner, but a more bitter pang was the thought that Wales was deprived of a long and steadfast friend, whose love of country had been something far more precious and real than an empty and vapid sentiment.[6]

It was intended to be a private occasion, but an invitation had been ex-

---

1   *Cymru, 1908/9* 'Gwenynen Gwent', L. M. Owen
2   *THSC* 'Lady Llanover and Her Circle', Maxwell Fraser
3   Probably Henrietta Maria Arianwen
4   Edward Bleiddian Herbert, 1858-1931
5   Lady Llanover's funeral took place on Thursday 23rd January 1896
6   *The Cardiff Times and South Wales Weekly News*

tended to all tenants who wished to be there. The hundreds who accepted the invitation found that there were ample refreshments for all, laid out in an outbuilding. The specially invited guests were given a 'sumptuous luncheon' in the mansion.

In the early afternoon of that sombre day the coffin was brought from the bedroom into the mansion's large hall. It was made of oak covered by a shell of lead, and the whole encased in Llanover oak from the same source as that used for Lord Llanover's coffin, having been carefully stored in the carpenter's workshop since His Lordship's death in 1867. Estate workers Elias Francis, Owen Lewis, *Madog Môn,* and Jones of Haymead [sic] Farm, Abergavenny, made Her Ladyship's coffin.

Truly, there was something remarkable in the fact that the three men who made her coffin bore on them clear marks of Wales. One was a harp-maker, another a chaired bard, and the other a penillion singer in the National Eisteddfod.[7]

Rhys Yr Ardd [Rees the Garden] laid the wreaths 'lovingly and artistically' on the coffin and the bier, giving a prominent place on the coffin lid to a magnificent arrangement of 'lilium harrissi and white lilac, beautifully entwined on a groundwork of azaleas and white tulips dotted with maiden hair fern', sent by Princess Mary Adelaide, Duchess of Teck.[8] The wreath from Lady Llanover's sister-in-law, Mrs Hall[9] of *Bryn Briallen*, Weston Park, Bath was made of jessamine, violets and narcissus

Among the many other floral tributes was a wreath of Christmas roses and snowdrops from Mrs Harford and the Misses Harford of Blaise Castle, Bristol and Falcondale, Lampeter. Mrs Harford was Lady Llanover's niece[10] who married John Battersby Harford. When writing to her niece at Falcondale, Lady

Falcondale, Lampeter

Image reproduced by kind permission of Chris and Lisa Hutton

---

7 *Cymru, 1908/9* 'Gwenynen Gwent', L. M. Owen
8 Princess Mary Adelaide, 1833-1897.
    Granddaughter of George III. Her daughter, Mary, was consort of King George V
9 Widow of Richard Crawshay Hall (1804-84), Lord Llanover's brother
10 Mary Charlotte Elizabeth Bunsen

Llanover would address the envelope *Cwm Curyll, Llanbedr-pont-Stephan, (miscalled Lampeter).*[11]

The Johnes family of Dolaucothi wrote on theirs *Mewn cof caredig am gyfeilles anwyl* [In fond memory of a dear friend]; and the wreath from the Llandovery School Trustees was sent ... *gyda chofion tyner am lawer o garedigrwydd* [... with tender memories of many kindnesses]. But perhaps the most appropriate tribute, 'which had reference to Lady Llanover's fondness for the melodies of Telyn Gwalia', was from Mrs Wellesley Pigott of Tedworth Square, and was in the shape of a harp.

The frame of the harp consisted of narcissus and the strings of blue violets, with a base of lilac and white azalea intermixed with asparagus fern and sprays of lily of the valley.[12]

When all was ready, the members of the household came slowly into the hall, the women dressed in 'tall chimney-pot hats over white caps, muslin aprons, and black turnovers.' Many had grown old in Her Ladyship's service and their tears fell freely as they walked slowly around the flower-strewn coffin.

After a short service on the terrace at the front of the house, the solemn procession began, led by the clergy. Among the pallbearers were Lord Tredegar, Sir James Hills-Johnes and Mr Morgan Williams of Aberpergwm. The coffin was carried the whole way on the shoulders of the tenants and more than twenty shared the task of carrying it on the slow, sorrowing

Llanover Hall
The Western Mail. Photograph: Moira Harry

walk along the path to the small church of St Bartholomew. Among them were *Rhys Yr Ardd*, Francis Harris of Dobson's Farm, Richard Morgan of Penty, John Munckley of Beiliglas, and W. E. Francis of *Tŷ Coch*. All the mourners were on foot, including the elderly Mrs Herbert, who leaned heav-

---

11 *The South Wales Squires*, H. M. Vaughan
12 *The South Wales Daily News*

ily on the arm of her son Ivor. She had recently become a widow, her husband, John Arthur Edward Herbert,[13] having died five months previously.

Lady Llanover's Funeral Procession
The Western Mail. Photograph: Moira Harry

Although sombre, the scene was picturesque. Many of the men were bare-headed for the whole distance, and there was not a vehicle to be seen. The women, dressed in Welsh costume, were each carrying a bunch of snowdrops, white roses and maidenhair fern, and the coffin, its brass fittings gleaming and its lid covered with beautiful flowers, was followed closely by the flower-strewn bier. For nearly an hour the choir sang sorrowful hymns while the cortège wended its way through the park, and so great was the number of mourners that not everyone was able to enter the Church. The burial service was conducted by Archdeacon Howell, *Llawdden,* whose emotion was clear for everyone to see. For many years he had been a loyal and steadfast friend to Lady Llanover, examining the schoolchildren for the annual prize given by Her Ladyship to the one showing the greatest proficiency in Welsh, and, together with Canon Sylvan Evans and Dr Saunders, compiling a Welsh Prayer Book for Lady Llanover's private use.

---

13 John Arthur Edward Herbert (formerly Jones), 1818-1895

Following the service the chief mourners and pall-bearers gathered at the tomb where, to the sound of the language so dear to her, the *Arglwyddes* was laid to rest at the side of her beloved Benjamin, sharing their final resting place with their son Hanbury and their grandson Stephan Sulien Herbert.

Llanofer Tomb

A simple Calvinistic Methodist service and the charming sad notes of their old hymns broke on the deep silence of her grave.[14]

'She has been a mother to us all', sighed a tearful, grey-haired manservant.

Col. Herbert received several deputations during the day. While expressing their sympathy to the bereaved family, they were anxious to know how their lives would be changed. They were sent away reassured that 'the traditions of Llanover in all matters Welsh shall be loyally and steadfastly maintained.'[15] Col. Herbert had inherited his late grandmother's love of Wales, although he had spent much of his adult life abroad. He entered the Grenadier Guards in 1870, and served in the Egyptian Campaign (1882), the Nile Expedition (1884-5), as Military Attaché at St Petersburg (1886-90) and as Commanding Officer of the Canadian Militia, with the local rank of Major-General. When the Militia were brought to the United Kingdom for Queen Victoria's Diamond Jubilee in 1897, Col. Herbert was placed in charge of them.

The newspapers printed many column inches recollecting the days when Lady Llanover was 'in the hey-day of her beauty and mental vigour and great social influence.'[16]

... the mere mention of her name called forth a host of memories of a past when the lady of Llanover was a personage of very great importance indeed ... Lord Llanover was immensely popular for his own manifest qualities, but his personality, great as it was, did not eclipse the equally great personality, in Wales at least, of Lady Llanover.[17]

---

14 *Cymru, 1908/9* 'Gwenynen Gwent', L. M. Owen
15 *The South Wales Daily News*
16 *The Western Mail*
17 *The Pontypool Free Press*

The South Wales Daily News recalled Her Ladyship's penchant for using Welsh names for people and places. Her letters to her chaplains began *Parchedig Sir,* [Reverend Sir]; her cream-coloured carriage ponies were *Cymro Bach* [Little Welshman] and *Cymro Mawr* [Big Welshman]; a goat was called *Caswallon*[18] and the housedog *Gofalus* [Careful]. Visitors to the mansion would be greeted with *Croesaw i Llanover; mae yma ymborth a lletty i chwi* [Welcome to Llanover; there is bed and board for you here]. One of the maids, from Glandovey, was called *Siân Dyfi*; the gardener was, as already mentioned, *Rhys Yr Ardd*; the blacksmith, – *Y Gof*; the boatman on the tiny ferry across the Usk was – *Y Badwr*. A favourite corner of the flower garden, *Yr Ardd Flodau*, was said to be the haunt of fairies, and was known as *Tylwyth Teg* [lit. Fair Family, that is, fairies].

Her Ladyship had a wonderful memory; she had a vast store of interesting anecdotes and she enjoyed 'recalling incidents of a hoary past.' One who had been associated with her work for a long time thought she was one of the cleverest women he had ever known. 'In stratagem,' he said, 'she might easily have outwitted a field-marshal.'

She was fiercely protective of the manuscripts in the library at Llanover. The Rev. T. C. Phillips and the Rev. Benjamin Williams, *Gwynionydd,* copied hundreds of proverbs from them to send to Canon Sylvan Evans when he was compiling his Welsh dictionary. Lady Llanover was subsidising this important work, which came to a standstill at her death. There was some concern regarding its completion but, thankfully, there was every hope that the Treasury would come to its rescue.

> *Mr. Balfour has been seen in connection with the matter, and it is believed on excellent authority that a grant will be made by the Treasury, and that the only point now to be decided is the form of the subsidy.*[19]

Her Ladyship was firmly of the opinion that Monmouthshire was in Wales and always addressed her letters home to Llanover, Monmouthshire, South Wales. On hearing someone state that Monmouthshire was, in a legal sense, an English county, Lady Llanover became very indignant and 'proceeded to show that it was simply included in the Oxford circuit for the convenience of the Bar of England.'[20] *Morien,*[21] writing in the *Western Mail,* stated:

---

18 *Caswallon,* a British chieftain in the time of Caesar
19 *The North Wales Chronicle*
20 *The Western Mail*
21 Owen Morgan, *Morien,* c.1836-1921, journalist

... had it been declared that Monmouthshire was not within the border of Wales it is almost certain that [Lady Llanover] would have removed from Llanofer and fixed her new abode within the recognised boundary of the kingdom of the Cymry.

Not long before her death Lady Llanover had related a story to Rev. Prys:

... how when a maiden in her teens she was on one occasion out for a ride, accompanied by one of her father's grooms, a sturdy Welshman, who, she explained, was magnificently arrayed in red plush knee-breeches. Welsh was even in those days showing evidence of decay in the district around, and this led the groom to remark with a sigh, 'What a pity it was to think that 40 years hence the Welsh would be an unknown language in these parts.' The young heiress instantly answered, 'You are wrong, for Welsh shall be very much spoken here if I can help it.' [22]

Her Ladyship encouraged ...

... every object calculated to give dignity and tone to Wales as a distinct nationality. The prize, annually made, to encourage the breeding of the native Welsh mountain sheep, those 'baa-baa black sheep, got any wool?' of nursery inquiry, is one of the incidents of Lord Tredegar's show, and also proof of her ladyship's constancy. [23]

She greatly admired these animals for the fine quality of their mutton and their milk, which made an excellent cheese, although ...

... in consequence of the non-encouragement, or rather the discouragement, of the old native Welsh cloth, and of hand-knit stockings, black wool was now sold in some places at a lower price than white; whereas, formerly black (very justly) always bore a higher price, in consequence of its superior value for stockings, and home-spun cloth, which, requiring no dye, was much more durable, and the tint of which could be made less intense, where desired, by mixing white wool with it. [24]

It seems that her Ladyship did not like having her photograph taken, although there is evidence that she was very interested in photography. [25] *The South Wales Daily News* told the story of the only photograph known to have been taken of Lady Llanover. She disliked it so much that it was never seen

---

22 See also Chapter 1
23 *The South Wales Daily News*
24 *First Principles of Good Cookery,* Lady Llanover
25 See a photograph album in GRO ref. MSS 1931

outside Llanover Court! The well-known portrait of her, 'characteristically attired in a red Welsh turnover, and wearing a sugar-loaf hat', was painted by Mornewick and a replica was commissioned, which was presented to Llandovery College by Lord Llanover.

Lady Llanover's will was dated 16th August 1889. Her executors were Col. Charles Lyne of Brynhyfryd, Newport, W. D. Freshfield of 5 Bank Buildings, and Abel John Ram of 3 Chester Square. Her Ladyship's personal estate was valued at £71,862 and was devised to trustees, namely W. D. Freshfield, and Abel John Ram, with Col. Lyne as managing trustee.

Lady Llanover's will contains throughout stringent provisions that no person professing the Roman Catholic religion, and not being a Protestant Trinitarian Christian, shall take any benefit under the will or succeed as a tenant to the settled estates, while the farm and cottage tenants are to be Welsh and able to speak the Welsh language, and every lease and agreement is to contain a provision for determination if the tenant shall become a Roman Catholic.[26]

All the effects at Llanover, the Abercarn mansion and 9 Great Stanhope Street were to become heirlooms and the trustees were to spend £1000 on furniture for the Colnbrook [sic] House as a place of residence for Henrietta Maria Arianwen Herbert, Lady Llanover's granddaughter.

Mrs Herbert was to be allowed to live at the mansions and the trustees were to maintain the properties and employ servants, all of whom were to be Protestant and Welsh-speaking.

Similar rights of residence were given to a granddaughter, grandson, and great-granddaughter successively, and there was an ultimate devise of the said freehold hereditaments to the daughters of her great-granddaughter by a Protestant Trinitarian husband successively in tail male.[27]

Llandovery School celebrated its fiftieth anniversary in 1897 and at the old boys' reunion in Cardiff the chairman, the Bishop of St Asaph,[28] spoke of Lady Llanover with affection and humour. He recalled an occasion, some years previously, when 'a candidate for the highest office which Llandovery could confer' was asked by Lady Llanover, the senior trustee, to visit her. After conversing for a while in Welsh they …

… lapsed into that vulgar speech called English - (laughter) - but before starting

---

26 *The Times*
27 *The Weekly Reporter*
28 Alfred George Edwards, 1848-1937

back on his journey she asked him whether he would have some tea. He replied in admirable Welsh that the 'pentrylliad' had offered him a cup of tea before!

The use of this word for butler so impressed her Ladyship that she wrote that although she had met many Welsh scholars, not one of them knew the Welsh word for butler. She thought therefore that this man must be a very great scholar! That, said the Bishop, marked a turning point in his career! He added that although leading Welsh clergy, bards and *literati* had visited her Ladyship, 'she had never met one who knew that "pentrylliad" was the Welsh for butler.'

This does not speak well of the Biblical knowledge of her Ladyship's visitors, for Pharaoh's butler, in the story of Joseph, is styled 'pentrylliad' in the Welsh version.'[29]

The main object of the founder of Llandovery School, Thomas Phillips, was ensuring that the pupils were instructed and educated in the Welsh language, and it was stipulated in the trust conditions that this was to be faithfully observed. At first this stipulation was complied with, but it was when the Bishop became warden that the founder's wishes were ignored. This caused a rift between the Bishop and Lady Llanover, although she remained a trustee in name.

Whatever be the merits of the dispute, it is at least strange to find the Bishop of St. Asaph setting the fashion in diverting endowments to other purposes than those intended by the pious founder.[30]

Rev. David Howell, Llawdden

In March that year the Venerable David Howell, *Llawdden,* was appointed to the deanery of St David's. This would have pleased Lady Llanover very much as she 'looked to "Llawdden" as her chief earthly guide, philosopher, and friend in all matters that pertained to Wales.'[31]

Queen Victoria celebrated her Diamond Jubilee in June 1897 with great pageantry. Huge crowds gathered overnight to watch the 'mightiest spectacular procession the world has ever seen' with many more people arriving with the dawn.

29 *The Western Mail*
30 *The Liverpool Mercury*
31 *The Western Mail*

159

... close upon fifty thousand soldiers, spick and span (and a finer body of troops no country could place upon a field or route), without fuss or offensive harshness to the people who lined the pavements, took up positions one pace from the kerb, drawing two clear red lines from Buckingham Palace to St. Paul's and onwards.'

Troops from all parts of the Empire had been brought to London for the occasion, and shortly after nine o'clock the procession of Colonial troops began. Field-Marshall Lord Roberts, Colonel-in-Chief, and Colonel Ivor Herbert, Colonel Commandant of the Colonial troops, led this fine body of men. So large was the contingent that it took twenty minutes to pass the stands where 'the souls of the multitude were stirred to the fever-point of enthusiasm.'[32] At the beginning of July these troops were reviewed by the Queen at Windsor. Over 900 officers and men left London by train and Colonel Herbert met them at Windsor station, from where he organised their march to the castle. During the review, he attended the Queen, together with Lord Roberts and Lord Methuen. The next day the troops were on parade again, this time at Buckingham Palace where they received their Commemoration medals from the Prince of Wales.

These men, with their colourful uniforms, had greatly entertained the crowds, and in return they were entertained at the theatre. On their behalf, Colonel Herbert accepted an invitation to a matinee performance of 'David Garrick' at the Criterion Theatre.[33] They also attended an afternoon performance at Her Majesty's Theatre where they were warmly welcomed by Mr Beerbohm Tree. Colonel Herbert was there, seated in the stalls with the other officers.[34]

It was also the year that the National Eisteddfod was held in Newport. Many had thought that the plans were too elaborate, that the pavilion was twice the size it need be, and others thought that changing the usual day of inauguration to a Monday left many

Gwenllian Llwyd carrying the Corn Hirlas

---

32 *The Pall Mall Gazette*
33 *The Daily News*
34 *The Era*

unaware of the change, hence the poor attendance.[35] However, *The Graphic* reported that in many ways it had been 'the most remarkable Eisteddfod of modern years.' Lord Tredegar gave the *Gorsedd* a model of the *Corn Hirlas* [Horn of Plenty] that he intended to present to them, and that he hoped to see used at future gatherings of the *Gorsedd*. Professor Herkomer had designed new outfits for the bards, which were 'given for their use as a gift "for ever" '.[36]

The proceedings once again were bilingual, which would not have pleased Lady Llanover, and she would have been very distressed at the popularity of the piano competitions compared with the harp contests.

Harp entries: Female	*3*
Male	*5*
Pedal Harp Solo	*12*
Triple Harp Solo	*3*
Junior Piano entries	*80*
Senior Piano entries	*74*[37]

The eighteen entries on the topic 'Wales's lament after the late Lady Llanover' would doubtless have made little impression on Her Ladyship; whatever efforts she made, however much money she spent, everything was for the benefit of *Cymru* and the *Cymry*[38] and not for personal glorification.

The choral competitions were always fiercely contested and the huge crowd, between 10,000 and 12,000 in number,[39] were restless and impatient for the performances to begin. Conditions were not good; the acoustics were poor and the pavilion very hot, but the audience gave each choir a warm reception, even the choir from North Wales being cheered again and again! If a choral competition result was unpopular with the audience, they could sometimes become rowdy and display their displeasure. Sir A. C. Mackenzie, who gave the adjudication at the 1897 Newport Eisteddfod, had been warned of this, and although nothing untoward was reported in the newspapers at the time, the following excerpt appeared in the Dowlais Male Choir's newsletter (date unknown).

The distinguished musician Sir Alexander Mackenzie had to be escorted to

---

35 *The Liverpool Mercury*
36 *The Welsh Spirit of Gwent*, Mair Elvet Thomas
37 *The Western Mail*
38 Wales and the Welsh people
39 *The Liverpool Mercury*

safety from an eisteddfod in Newport in 1897.

On the last day a resolution was passed 'to petition the Queen that an arms representing Wales should be introduced into the Royal shield and coinage and that the emblem of Wales might be added to the National Flag.'[40]

Mrs Herbert played only a small part at this Eisteddfod – she gave a pound each to two runners-up in the competition for penillion with the harp.

A year later she announced the marriage of her daughter, Henrietta, to the Hon. Walter Constable Maxwell.[41] The ceremony took place at St John's Roman Catholic Church in Bath on the 24th November 1898. Henrietta was nearly 50 years old and Walter four years younger.

The weather was unusually favourable for the National Eisteddfod when it was held in Cardiff in 1899. According to *The Liverpool Mercury* this eisteddfod 'went deeper and passed beyond the geographical boundaries of Wales, and included representatives of the other branches of the Celtic race from Scotland, Ireland and Brittany.' Representatives from the Isle of Man were also present. Mrs Herbert gave her support by lending some paintings to the Eisteddfod museum, namely, portraits of Lady Llanover, *Carnhuanawc* and *Gruffydd,* and by giving a prize of one guinea to a lad named Robert Evans of Abertillery, who was placed second in the violin solo competition for under sixteen-year-olds. Also, she invited the Breton delegates to visit her at Llanover at the end of the week.

The *Corn Hirlas* promised by Lord Tredegar in 1897 was presented to the *Gorsedd.* It was 'of the pattern in vogue among ancient British Kings …really a princely present'.[42] It had been designed by Goscombe John, the Welsh sculptor, and 'made with silver and set with precious stones.'[43] That horn was still in use almost 90 years later, in 1988, when the National Eisteddfod again visited Newport.[44]

There were eight entries for the pedal harp solo. The prize of three guineas and a gold medal, given by Erard for the best performance of 'Pensive and Joyous' by John Thomas, *Pencerdd Gwalia,* was awarded to Master James Williams of Abergavenny who 'was an easy winner.' Sadly, although there were seven entries for the triple harp solo, only one competitor turned up! It

---

40 *The Graphic*
41 Walter Constable Maxwell, 1852-1925
42 *The Western Mail*
43 *The Glasgow Herald*
44 *The Welsh Spirit of Gwent*, Mair Elvet Thomas

was Miss Maggie Jones of Newbridge, Monmouthshire. Dr Parry thought her playing good enough to award her the prize of three guineas. When giving the adjudication, Dr Parry also said:

> ... *[he] deprecated the spirit of criticism which would send to oblivion the national instrument of Wales – the triple harp. (Applause.) Its use had been fostered by the late Lady Llanover – (Applause) – and he hoped and believed her daughter, the Hon Miss Hubert [sic] – who was present that day - would lend her countenance to the fostering of the triple harp of Wales. (Applause.)*[45]

On the Saturday, after a breakfast given by Lord Windsor, a large party of Celtic delegates and eisteddfod officials left Cardiff by train for Abergavenny, en route to Llanover. They were met at Abergavenny and 'conveyed in three breaks' to Llanover. When they passed through Llanellen the Bretons were very interested in the name of the inn – *Seren Gobaith*[46] [Star of Hope]:

> ... *which betokened that the domain of Llanover had been entered; and the vehicles stopped at the North Gate of the park (called Porth Mawr Llanofer) to allow the visitors to read and copy the Welsh inscriptions of welcome and Godspeed inscribed on either side over the archway.*[47]

Visitors entering the park saw the words:

Pwy wyt ti Ddyfodwr? [Who are you, comer?]

Os cyfaill, croesaw calon i ti; [If friend, the welcome of the heart to thee;]

Os dieithr, lleteugarwch a'th erys; [If stranger, hospitality shall meet thee;]

Os gelyn, addfwynder a'th garchara. [If enemy, courtesy shall imprison thee.]

And when leaving they saw:

Ymadawydd hynaws! [Departing guest!]

Gad dy fendith ar dy ol, a bendithier dithau. [Leave a blessing on thy footsteps and mayst thou be blessed.]

Iechyd a hawddfyd it' ar dy daith [Health and prosperity be with thee on thy journey]

A dedwydd dychweliad.[48][And happiness on thy return.]

The delegates' journey resumed through the long, shady avenues that led to the front of the mansion. Mrs Herbert was in the hall to meet the visitors

---

45 *The Western Mail*

46 *Seren Gobaith* – originally the Red Lion

47 *The Western Mail*

48 *Cymru, 1908/9* 'Gwenynen Gwent', L. M. Owen

while the family harper played the 'March of the Men of Harlech'. Then they were taken to see the Nine Wells, 'a deliciously cool grot [sic] in a grove of ancient elms.'

At luncheon, Mrs Herbert sat at one end of the table and her son Ivor at the other. Speeches of thanks from some of the Breton gentleman were made, to which Ivor replied, in French, on his mother's behalf …

… saying how great was her pleasure at taking that opportunity of following the traditions of Llanover in showing hospitality to the Celts of Brittany and to lovers of the Welsh nationality.

Susanna Berrington
Gruffydd Richards

Image reproduced by kind permission
of Mr. T. F. James

Then the guests were entertained by Mrs Gruffydd Richards singing old Welsh songs to her own accompaniment 'on the old triple-stringed harp, an inscription on which showed that it was made at Cardiff by Bassett Jones in 1839.' Most of the party left soon afterwards, the others remaining at Llanover for a few days. At half past eight on the Sunday morning the Bretons, with Mrs Herbert and her other Catholic visitors, attended mass in the chapel of Llanover House. After breakfast some of them walked across the park to *Tŷ Uchaf* to inspect 'the ancient harpsichord on which Handel once played.'[49] *Morien* was among the guests 'through the kindness of Mrs. Herbert', and while the others were at mass on that lovely Sunday morning he wandered in 'the haunts of the *Tylwyth Teg.*' He wrote of the feeling of sorrow there:

… because the venerable 'Gwenynen Gwent' is no longer here in the flesh as in other days to say 'Groesaw i Llanover'. But in the midst of a strain of melancholy one is somehow strongly impressed with an indefinable consciousness that the spirit of the departed august 'Arglwyddes' is still here.

Mrs Herbert explained to him her reason for inviting the Bretons to Llanover; she felt certain that 'her doing so would have been highly pleasing

---

49 Mrs Delany mentioned her 'little spinnet', [similar to a harpsichord] on which Handel played

to her departed parents, Lord and Lady Llanover.'

Dr Parry's plea that Mrs Herbert 'would lend her countenance to the fostering of the triple harp' struck a chord with her! She very soon began making enquiries through Dafydd Watts, who seems to have taken over some of Dafydd Williams's work when the latter moved to Cardiff, about 1889.

Letters[50] were sent to Welsh harpers and schoolmasters asking them to let him know, as soon as possible, of any Welsh harpers in their neighbourhood.

One of the first to reply was James Williams,[51] Dafydd Williams's son, who, in the 1895 Kelly's Directory, was referred to as 'Welsh Harpist'. He responded to the enquiry immediately. He played the triple harp, but knew of no one else who did, and the only triple harp he knew of was his own! This is surprising as he and his sister, Elizabeth Ann,[52] had both been members of Lady Llanover's band of harpists; she, now married with a small daughter,[53] was also living in Cardiff.

Mary Pearce, of Treherbert, replied on behalf of her late husband, *Telynwr [sic] y Bryniau* [Harper of the Hills]. In her area she only knew of two triple harpers, namely, her sons, Ap Pearce and Rosser Pearce. She mentioned that their triple harp had been made in a place near Abergavenny.

John Bryant of Efail Isaf replied, although he only played the double action pedal harp. However, he was a Welsh speaker. He did not know of any triple harp players in South Wales, but had heard of someone named Roberts in North Wales. This could have been John L. Roberts, *Telynor Maldwyn,* from Builth Wells who replied to Dafydd Watts promptly saying that he could speak Welsh quite well, but could neither read nor write the language. He played both the triple-stringed harp and the 'English' harp. His brother Albert also spoke Welsh and played the triple harp. Others he knew of in North Wales were the Jones family of Llannerchymedd,[54] but he knew of no one in the South.

The Jones family of the Britannia Inn, Llannerchymedd were harpers of some note. John Jones wrote to Dafydd Watts proudly listing the harpers in the family and their successes. He, *Telynor Môn,* had three sons; Owen, *Telynor Seiriol;* Robert, *Telynor Cymreig;* and William, *Telynor Gwalia.* He remarked that

---

50 GRO Ref. D1210.827

51 The author's great-uncle

52 See Chapter 5

53 Mary Ayrona, who was later taught to play the triple harp

54 See *Telynorion Llannerch-y-medd,* Huw Roberts and Llio Rhydderch. (Bilingual)

these three had won prizes given by Lady Llanover at the Swansea Eisteddfod about twelve years previously. Also, the three had been successful at the Caerwys National Eisteddfod, and *Telynor Seiriol* had played before the Prince of Wales at the Caernarfon National Eisteddfod. John Jones's brother, Owen Jones, *Owain Môn,* of Rhosgoch, was also an accomplished triple harper, as was his daughter, Ellen Jane, *Telynores Cybi.* Between them they had many prizes as proof of their successes playing the triple harp. He knew of Robert Jones, Llangollen, someone by the name of Woods in Corwen, and a Roberts in Newtown. The latter was probably John Roberts, [55] *Telynor Cymru;* five of his thirteen children learned to play the triple harp and the family had given a concert before Queen Victoria at Palé Hall, Merioneth.[56]

Robert Jones, of Llangollen, wrote to Dafydd Watts informing him that he spoke Welsh and played the triple harp. He had played at the Hand Hotel in Llangollen during the summer season for 37 years but he did not know of any other Welsh musicians in that neighbourhood. He still did his best in spite of suffering from pain and weakness in both hands, which badly affected his playing. The previous year he had the honour of meeting Mrs Herbert when she was at Plas Madryn

E. Wood-Jones, *Telynor Meirion,* was the brother of John Jones, the Llanover family harper, who had died many years before and was buried in the churchyard at St Bartholomew's. He was proud to say that he was a warm-hearted Welshman, able to speak Welsh and to play the triple harp and as far as he knew, he was the only one in North Wales to play the old national instrument! He had recently had the honour of playing for the Prince of Wales at Ruthin Castle, and he would be honoured to be of service to Mrs Herbert at any time.

Within a few weeks Mr Watts had prepared a list for Mrs Herbert. Added to those already mentioned were the names of Mrs Gruffydd Richards and Robert McKirdy[57] of Cardiff.

Many years before this, Ellis Roberts, *Eos Meirion,* had written a volume of exercises for the triple harp, which had won first prize at the Llangollen Eisteddfod of 1858.[58] The manuscript had been lost for many years and when it was rediscovered Mrs Herbert played a part in its being published in 1902,

---

55 See Chapter 5
56 Queen Victoria visited Palé Hall in 1889
57 See Chapter 5
58 *Arglwyddes Llanofer, Gwenynen Gwent,* Rachel Ley

saying in the introduction that now no one had an excuse for saying there was not a book for teaching the instrument, and that she hoped that the playing of it would increase quickly. However, the exercises used in the book were taken from those of Bochsa and so were not much help in dealing with the complication of trying to cope with the middle row of strings.[59] Mrs Herbert also encouraged triple harpers to come to Llanover for tuition with Mrs Gruffydd Richards. Writing about *Gwenynen Gwent* in 1908,[60] L. M. Owen remarked that at that time triple harps were still being made at Llanover.

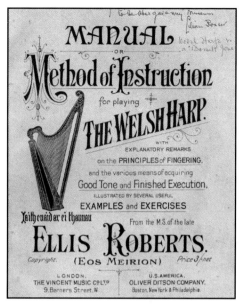

Ellis Roberts' Manual

Image reproduced by kind permission of Monmouthshire County Council, Abergavenny Museum

Col. Herbert was well respected by his Llanarth tenants and he received a very warm welcome home when he returned from South Africa at the end of December 1900. His response to the addresses he received was in Welsh, showing that he had inherited his grandmother's love of the language. His role in South Africa as assistant adjutant-general to Lord Kitchener was one of great responsibility and although he was not involved in the fighting, his life was put in danger from an unexpected source.

Mrs Richard Chamberlain, sister-in-law of the Colonial Secretary, had spent several months in South Africa and had worked in a hospital in Cape Town. On her return to London she was interviewed by a London News Agency and her comments were scathing! The hospital building was in a beautiful location, but no attempt had been made to clean it before the wounded men were admitted. This resulted in the patients having 'to be covered in insect powder to keep off the vermin.' The situation was reported to the military authorities who did nothing! There was just one nursing sister to 175 men. Many sisters had gone to Cape Town from Johannesburg, wanting to work, 'but the authorities preferred to let the men die ... rather than employ these women.' The orderlies were good and there were plenty of

---

59 *Arglwyddes Llanofer, Gwenynen Gwent,* Rachel Ley
60 *Cymru, 1908/9* 'Gwenynen Gwent', L. M. Owen

them, but they were not organised properly.

> *[Utensils] which had been used for typhoid patients were indiscriminately given to other patients. Now, there was no reason whatever why any of these disgraces should have existed. There was plenty and to spare of everything if it had been allowed to be distributed.*[61]

Mrs Chamberlain was of the opinion that most of the army doctors 'were of a low class of men' with little knowledge of the most basic sanitary rules. They abused their authority and neglected their patients in spite of all the civilian doctors tried to do to improve the situation. Officers and men suffered alike. One young man, Mrs Chamberlain's youngest brother, was maimed for life through being 'left ten days without having his knee set', and Col. Herbert was given thirty times the prescribed dose of arsenic, which almost killed him!

> *Arsenic poisoning is not confined to this country. Colonel Ivor Herbert, who had a warm Welsh welcome home at Llanarth on Monday, was poisoned with an overdose of arsenic in South Africa, administered by misadventure.*[62]

After her mother's death Mrs Herbert 'had continuously resided in one or other' of the mansions. Was she finding it irksome to live under the conditions of her mother's will? In May 1897 *The Times* published a brief notice, as follows:

> *Lord Chancellor's Court – Before Mr. Justice Fabwill at 10.30. Re Baroness Llanover (Herbert v. Freshfield) part heard.*

In July the same year *The Daily News* published, under the heading LAW NOTICES: Chancery Division, Court 1. Before Mr Justice North. Re: Lady Llanover (Freshfield v. Herbert).

There were reports in *The Times* in 1902 and *The Weekly Reporter* in 1903 regarding a summons taken out by Mrs Herbert against the trustees of the Llanover estate to determine her status; was she a 'tenant for life within the meaning of the Settled Land Acts'? thus having the powers of a tenant for life over 'certain mansion-houses and land settled by the will.' The hearing was held before Mr Justice Swinfen Eady who decided in Mrs Herbert's favour.

> *It might be that the result would have surprised the testatrix and was contrary to her intention, but the Settled Land Acts did override testators' intentions.*

---

61 *The Northern Echo*
62 *The Western Mail*

The trustees realised that this ruling was indeed contrary to Lady Llanover's wishes and appealed against the decision. This was heard by the Master of the Rolls, Lord Justice Romer and Lord Justice Cozens-Hardy, and after representations from Mr Haldance, KC and Mr Howard Wright for the trustees, and Mr Warmington, KC and Mr H. Fellows for Mrs Herbert, the appeal was dismissed. The trustees were ordered to pay Mrs Herbert's costs 'but without prejudice to the question from what source the costs were to be defrayed.'[63]

It is interesting to note that on the night the 1901 census was taken there were 12 people at Llanover Court, 10 of whom were Welsh speaking, the remaining two being upholsterers, one from London and the other from Paris. By the time the 1911 census was taken there were ten people living there, but only two of them were Welsh speakers! On both occasions Mrs Herbert was at 9 Great Stanhope Street, London.

In her article written in 1908, L. M. Owen admitted that although she had heard the name *Gwenynen Gwent,* she knew nothing of the life of Lady Llanover, thinking that maybe she had been a distinguished author who lived in some remote part of Wales. Ms Owen had been taught the history of English authors at school and had read about French and German authors, but it was not thought worth teaching them about the well-known people of Wales! The article was written after a great deal of research, and covered almost every aspect of Lady Llanover's love of Wales.

Mrs Herbert inherited many of her mother's attributes. Writing about 'The Lady of Llanover' H. M. Vaughan admits that he never met Lady Llanover, but had stayed there with her daughter, Mrs Herbert. He described her as 'a charming old lady, courteous and cultivated.'

Mrs. Herbert, when I knew her, was a very old lady, but as she dyed her abundant hair with henna, which produces a sort of geranium red tint, her appearance was somewhat remarkable. I remember years ago watching a queue of interested children following her about the Florentine churches, and speculating as to her hair. Mrs. Herbert was, however, well aware of the effect produced on the public by her dyed chevelure, but always asserted she was fully justified therein, for that was the exact colour of her hair when a girl, a rare shade of scarlet auburn.[64]

---

63 *The Times*
64 *The South Wales Squires,* H. M. Vaughan

Pedr James (inset) and his Triple Harp,
which he made himself.

Images reproduced by kind permission of Mrs Sue Hardie

She showed her willingness to continue the traditions of Llanover by making arrangements for a band of triple harpists to be present at the National Eisteddfod in Abergavenny in 1913. By this time she was 88 years old, and, sadly, she died a few months before the event. Her funeral was held at Llanover, where the hall of the mansion had been made a temporary chapel for the Requiem Mass, celebrated by the Bishop of Newport.[65] Tenants and workmen bore her coffin to St Bartholomew's churchyard where she was buried.

Mrs Gruffydd Richards continued to prepare the harpers for the occasion. They were Stanley Jones, *Telynor y Bryniau,* Theresa Monkley, of Gilwern, Llyfni Huws, Mrs M. Davies, of Pontnewynydd, Enid Walters, Llanover, Pedr James, Llanover, Laura Jones, of Cerrigydrudion, and Dafydd Roberts, *Telynor Mawddwy.*

This support of the triple harp aroused once more the conflict between those supporting the old instrument and those favouring the pedal harp.[66]

---

65 *The Times*
66 *Arglwyddes Llanofer, Gwenynen Gwent,* Rachel Ley

Captain the Hon Elidyr Herbert (left)
(on the right is Gerry Horlick, whose family supplied
their famous drink to the troops during WW1)
Image reproduced by kind permission of Col. Rollo Clifford

Theresa Monckley's Harp
Image reproduced by kind permission of
Monmouthshire County Council,
Abergavenny Museum

In 1916 Sir Ivor Herbert,[67] who was elected Member of Parliament for South Monmouthshire in 1906, deposited the precious contents of the library at Llanover at the National Library of Wales, when it opened in Aberystwyth in 1916. In 1917 he became Baron Treowen of Treowen and Llanarth. His son, Elidyr, was a barrister and a justice of the peace, and like so many other young men he served in the First World War, as a Captain in the Royal Gloucester Hussars.

The grave of Captain Elidyr Herbert
Gaza Cemetery
Image reproduced by kind permission
of the British Consulate, Egypt

He was seconded to the Machine Gun Corps (Cavalry) and lost his life in action in Palestine on 12th November 1917. He is buried in Gaza War Cemetery.

---

67 Ivor Herbert became a baronet in 1907

Elidyr John Bernard Herbert, Yeomanry, was reported wounded and missing and subsequently reported in November 1917 to have been killed in Palestine ... He was awarded the Serbian Order of the White Eagle in 1916.[68]

In the 1920s Lord Treowen built *Tre Elidyr* [Elidyr's Town] in memory of his only son and the other brave young men of Llanover who had sacrificed their lives serving their country. By the time of his own death, in 1933, Llanover Court had been empty and decaying for some years.

The huge mansion was very expensive to maintain and to bring it up to date would have cost a fortune. There was a six-day sale of its contents in June 1934, and in 1935 the once grand mansion, scene of so many magnificent house parties, but also much sadness, was demolished.

J. C. Griffith-Jones visited Llanover in May 1935 and wrote a piece for *The News Chronicle* under the heading 'Silent Harp of Llanover.' He spoke to Sir John Herbert,[69] who told him of 'his dreams of restoring some of the magic of Welsh customs and Welsh colour which has been lost even to Llanofer' and he and his wife[70] were both anxious to learn Welsh. Major Herbert had been searching throughout Wales for a 'family harpist', without success. A brilliant young harpist had been recommended, 'but his "second string" was pharmacy' and Llanover needed a craftsman who was a harpist, in order to fit in with life on the estate.

The Garden at Tŷ'r Eglwys
Photograph: Ros Jeffries

Griffith-Jones then went to *Tŷ'r Eglwys* [Church House] to visit Mrs Gruffydd Richards, 'the strongest surviving link with the Llanover of colourful yesterdays.' They sat in her lovely garden while she talked wistfully of the old days. She was then 81 years old, and her eyesight was failing.

She explained that

---

68 King's College Annual Report
69 Sir John Herbert, 1895-1943
70 Mary Theresa Fox-Strangways, 1903-1948

the traditional Welsh instrument was the triple harp, and Welsh music had been composed especially for it, but sadly there was hardly anyone left who 'could play it or understand its difficult but beautiful semi-tones.' Her hundred-year-old harp was brought to her, its strings broken.

Rhes Ganol
Photograph: Rhes Ganol

She sat there in the sunshine with bowed head, her wan fingers caressing the beloved instrument drawing out of imaginary strings rich chords of lost harmonies.[71]

The triple harp, almost unknown in South Wales in the 1940s, is experiencing a new lease of life. Thanks to the likes of Dr Nancy Richards Jones, in the North there is an unbroken link to the ancient harpers of Wales. Both Llio Rhydderch and Robin Huw Bowen are present-day exponents of this traditional instrument, passing on the tradition to future generations. For the first time since the 1913 Abergavenny Eisteddfod a 'band' of triple harpists has been formed.[72]

By 1988, when the National Eisteddfod returned to Newport, the Welsh language had 'made leaps and bounds in some parts of Gwent …'

Gwent has always been part of Welsh cultural history despite fluctuations in the number of its Welsh population. A new beginning has been made in earnest and it has kindled hope for Gwent both inside the county and

71 *The News Chronicle*
72 *Rhes Ganol,* Robin Huw Bowen, Huw Roberts, Rhiain Bebb, Wynn Thomas and Steffan Thomas

throughout the rest of Wales.[73]

Unfortunately, at the National Eisteddfod in Denbigh in 2001, there was 'an ugly eruption of Welsh nationalism'.[74] Intemperate remarks were made, such as 'Wales has become a "dumping ground" for England's oddballs, social misfits and society drop-outs', and one person demanded that there should be a limit on the numbers of English people allowed to buy homes in Wales. The writer of the article, Lady Llanover's three times great-granddaughter, wondered what her energetic, crusading ancestor would have made of these rows.

Somehow, I can't see her wringing her hands and blaming the Welsh predicament on 'incomers', still less singing the song of hatred. No, she would be out with her hat and her harpist minting new 'traditions' as fast as the old ones fell from use: a magnificent English oddball on a mission to save the Welsh, not just from outsiders, but from themselves.

---

73 *The Welsh Spirit of Gwent,* Mair Elvet Thomas
74 *The Sunday Telegraph,* article by Susannah Herbert